NO OTHER WEALTH

The Prayers of a Modern-Day Saint
Bishop Charles Henry Brent
1862-1929

Edited by

FREDERICK WARD KATES

with a biographical memoir by

The Right Reverend Malcolm Endicott Peabody

Frederick Ward Kates

The Upper Room

The World's Most Widely Used Devotional Guide
and
Other Devotional Literature
1908 Grand Avenue
Nashville, Tennessee 37203

Library of Congress
Catalog Number: 65-18870

UR-207-15-0465
Printed in the United States of America

CHARLES HENRY BRENT
1862-1929

Bishop of the Philippine Islands
1901-1918

Bishop of Western New York
1918-1929

A Servant of God

A Friend of Humanity

An Apostle of Christian Unity

Chief of Chaplains, American Expeditionary
Force—1917-1919

President First World Conference on
Faith and Order—1927

—Inscription on his gravestone
Bois de Vaux Cemetery, Lausanne

While Anglicanism in particular and the Church of God in general can produce a character of the nobility, purity, courage, simplicity and achievement of Charles Henry Brent, no one need have any fears as to the future of the Christian religion.

—S. Parkes Cadman, 1864-1936
American Congregationalist clergyman

In Tribute

to

All who made "pilgrimage Godward" with
Bishop Brent in the Philippines, during
World War I, and in "Faith and Order"

"That he is with us no longer to lead is a
call to us all to follow more closely his
invisible leader."

—Alfred Ernest Garvie, 1861-1945
Bishop Brent's Deputy at Lausanne, 1927

EDITOR'S FOREWORD

Really to know a man is to pay heed to his prayers. The study of a man's prayers is a more effective avenue to a knowledge of what he was and what he sought to become than the most exhaustive biography. Held by this conviction, I have prepared this little volume of all the written prayers of Bishop Charles Henry Brent. In these pages, churchmen of this present generation will be able to discover what sort of man he was, this modern-day saint and mighty leader in Christendom during the first three decades of the twentieth century. Few men of his own generation touched life more relevantly and at so many points, and few men of his time lived more fully and participated more directly in the events of those stirring years. Bishop Brent lived in his own time, indeed; but he also lived ahead of it and beyond it.

The objects of his concern, labor, and love are set forth in his prayers; and also, by means of them, we who aspire to carry on where he pioneered the way are enabled to gain an understanding, otherwise denied, of the temper, fiber, and character of this exciting and noble leader of men.

It was Bishop Brent's habit to pray "pen in hand," and it is an awesome experience to trace in his diaries and notebooks many of his prayers day by day taking a final form. Phrase by phrase and line by line, the prayers assumed their final shape, after being hammered out in daily prayer. It was Bishop Brent's conviction that "an artistic prayer, a prayer carefully prepared, so far from being less is more spiritual by

7

virtue of its literary finish." Effort and care went into the fashioning of the prayers in the following pages.

Many of the prayers in this first complete collection of Bishop Brent's prayers have appeared in print since they were composed in the years between 1902 and 1929, but one fourth of them are here published for the first time. The ultimate source of the prayers in this collection and also of the data regarding dates of composition is the rich treasure of personal papers, letters, diaries, notebooks, sermon notes, and personal memorabilia of Bishop Brent now in permanent custody of the Manuscript Division of the Library of Congress, Washington, D.C. Identified as "The Bishop Charles Henry Brent Papers," the collection consists of approximately 13,540 items. Literary rights in the unpublished writings of Charles Henry Brent in the collection, as in other collections of manuscript material in the custody of the Library of Congress, have been dedicated to the public.

So here they are—Bishop Brent's prayers, the petitions and aspirations of an authentic Christian spirit who believed, "Those alone labor effectively among men who impetuously fling themselves upward toward God." All are marked by the free and ingenuous phrasing that flowed from his easy and unstrained approach to God, and all betray his lifelong passion for adventure in the divine and his desire to be rendered a fit instrument for the doing of God's will. Originally written in his diaries and notebooks or on random sheets of paper or on the blank pages at the back of material he was reading, the prayers of Bishop

Brent enable us to have our fingers on the pulse of his daily walking with God and to gain a new and true understanding of a fundamentally shy and austere yet splendidly virile man, who was an ascetic by training and a mystic by temperament.

May these prayers of a great Christian help us on our way as we make our pilgrimage Godward.

—FREDERICK WARD KATES

SOURCES AND ACKNOWLEDGMENTS

Twenty-six of the prayers in this book were published originally in *With God in Prayer* by Charles H. Brent, George W. Jacobs and Company, Philadelphia, 1907, a little volume now many years out of print and even beyond copyright. These prayers are: 3, 5, 9, 15-19, 20, 23, 24, 27, 49, 62, 67, 70, 80, 86, 88, 97, 98, 101, 124, 139, 145, 154. I wish to thank Macrae Smith Company, Philadelphia, for their permission to use these prayers in the present book.

Seventy-six of the numbered prayers in this book appeared in print in *Adventures in Prayer—Selected Prayers of Bishop Charles H. Brent*, edited by S. S. Drury, Harper & Brothers, New York, 1932, a book long out of print. Twenty of the prayers in the collection edited by S. S. Drury first appeared in print in *With God in Prayer* (1907). The other prayers in the present volume which also appear in Drury's collection are: 1, 2, 4, 6-8, 12, 14, 21, 25, 26, 28, 35, 36, 44, 48, 51, 58, 60, 61, 63, 66, 71, 75-79, 81, 89-92, 94-96, 107, 108, 110, 119, 122, 126, 130, 133, 135, 138, 141, 144, 147, 149, 151, 157, 158, 162, 165, 172. Thirteen of the prayers in sections 4 and 5 were also published in *Adventures in Prayer*. Harper & Row, Publishers, has graciously granted the editor of this book permission to use the above material.

Forty-eight prayers in the present volume were published in *Things That Matter—The Best of the Writings of Bishop Brent*, edited with a biographical sketch by Frederick W. Kates, Harper & Brothers, New York, 1949, pp. 61-89. All these prayers appeared first in the two titles mentioned above or were found in the unpublished literary material of Bishop Brent.

Harper & Row, Publishers, has granted permission to reprint in *No Other Wealth* prayers that were printed in *Things That Matter*.

The material on prayer used to introduce each section is from the writings of Bishop Brent.

Literary rights in the unpublished writings of Bishop Brent used in this volume have been given to the public by the Library of Congress, Washington, D.C., in whose possession, on permanent deposit and in permanent custody, are the literary remains of Bishop Brent in the Manuscript Division. These are identified as "The Bishop Charles Henry Brent Papers."

CONTENTS

NO OTHER WEALTH

The two great prizes of human life are fellowship with God and in Him fellowship with one another. There is no other wealth. The dimensions of fellowship—height: high as God; breadth: broad as the human race; depth: deep as our capacity.

—1927 Notebook

His magic was not far to seek—
He was so human! Whether strong or weak,
Far from his kind he neither sank nor soared,
But sate an equal guest at every board:
No beggar ever felt him condescend,
No prince presume; for still himself he bare
At manhood's simple level, and where'er
He met a stranger, there he left a friend.

                    —James Russell Lowell

THE RIGHT REVEREND CHARLES HENRY BRENT
1862-1929

A BIOGRAPHICAL MEMOIR
OF BISHOP BRENT

by

The Right Reverend Malcolm Endicott Peabody

Editor's Note—Bishop Peabody, who retired in 1960 after eighteen years of service as Bishop of the Diocese of Central New York, served under Bishop Brent as a missionary and master of the Baguio School in the Philippine Islands from 1911 until 1913, following his graduation in 1911 from Harvard College. He went overseas as a Red Cross chaplain in 1917, assigned to United States Base Hospital #5. In 1918 he transferred to the U. S. Army as a chaplain with the American Expeditionary Force in France and found himself again under Bishop Brent's jurisdiction and personal and paternal oversight. Since his consecration as Bishop in 1938, he has worn Bishop Brent's pectoral cross.

————————

Bishop Brent was known throughout the whole Christian Church as the great proponent of Christian unity of his time. Those who knew him as a friend, however, will testify that his greatness as a public figure was built upon his practice of prayer and the vision which grew out of it.

My experience of him dates from the year I got through college. My father, who observed that I had no special bent as yet, proposed my spending a year at Baguio School in the Philippines. At the same time he made an offer of my services to Bishop Brent, which the Bishop fortunately accepted. The turning point in my life dated from this acceptance.

During the two years that I spent in Baguio, the Bishop treated me as a son, let me make his house my headquarters in Manila, guided my faltering thoughts into intellectual and religious channels, and took me with him on a tour of the Islands in the summer of 1912. As he was the friend and pastor of every missionary he encountered, I had the privilege of observing his sympathy for churchmen of every branch in the Church. They laid their problems before him and looked upon him in a very real sense as their father in God.

Baguio School, now known as Brent School, provided the scene for my decision to enter the ministry. I had no inkling of this turn that affairs were taking in my innermost thoughts until, with unheralded suddenness, the decision came upon me, as it were, ready-made one morning. While my whole life, in a sense, had led up to this decision, the letter which I received from Bishop Brent at about this critical moment unconsciously must have prepared my mind and opened my spirit:

Of course I hope that you are going to find your vocation in the Ministry. As the years go on the splendor of its opportunity seems to increase. I wish I could begin all fresh in the new generation of clergy. They have the best and greatest before them of all men who have ever lived. The problems are more complex but the incentive to service is so wonderful as to make the whole man tingle. When you come to your decision, "live in the top story" of your verdict, and never look back. I imagine most men reach the sense of vocation only in part by thought. It is consummated by the act which finally commits us to a course. There is always an element of faith in it. But after the decision there comes an illumination which, I suppose, is one to spiritual obedience. Most professions are reached because of a certainty of knowledge as to gifts and achievements which leaves room for only a minimum of doubt. But in the case of the Ministry where the spiritual plays so prominent a part, there must perforce be a larger element of faith than ordinarily is called for. If a man is absolutely true to his first instincts he is not likely to make a mistake.

It was typical of him that he should have expressed himself with such loving care. It reflected, without doubt, the result of his own prayers in my behalf. The influence which he had on many souls, especially of young men, is thus illustrated as thoroughly typical of the personal care he gave to hundreds of people who crossed his path.

Several years later when I was changing over from a Red Cross chaplaincy to a chaplaincy in the U. S. Army, I stayed with him at Chaumont, where as Chaplain-General he lived at General Pershing's headquarters. It seemed odd to find this loving pastor in army uniform until I recollected that he had been a soldier of Christ in the literal sense from the first day he set foot in the Philippines.

One experience of this militant missionary revealed his aggressiveness in action as well as his submissiveness to God in quite a typical way. Eleanor Slater describes it in these vivid terms in her book *Charles Henry Brent—Everybody's Bishop:*

19

He could go where others could not go, do what others could not do, fight for order with his friendliness better than other men could fight for it with guns. When the American Governor was anxious to come to terms with a notorious band of outlaws, an armed ship and a little boat went out to meet the adversary on the appointed day—the one a symbol of force, the other a symbol of persuasion. But before the native boats would gather to the rendezvous, the armed ship had to steam away and leave the little boat to go alone upon its perilous errand. In it were Bishop Brent and his co-worker, Mrs. Lorillard Spencer, who met alone, unarmed, the most desperate of the Moro pirates, who swarmed onto their small boat armed and plotting murder. The story of what followed is told by Dr. Remsen Ogilby: Bishop Brent stood up in his little boat, took his penknife out of his pocket, and threw it down on the deck. "You call yourselves brave men," he said, pointing to his knife. "There is the only weapon I have. You come aboard my boat in the presence of an unarmed white man and a defenceless white woman, you, my guests, all armed to the teeth." One by one, we are told, the Moros, shamefaced, put down their weapons on the deck. Courage and courtesy had won.*

His capacity to dare boldly, however, was founded on his complete commitment by a mastery in the life of prayer which has been given only to God's saints. Remsen Ogilby, his great friend, told me that when Brent was at Saint Stephen's Church in South Boston, he would spend many hours of the night in prayers

---

* Eleanor Slater, *Charles Henry Brent—Everybody's Bishop.* Morehouse Publishing Co., Milwaukee, 1932, pages 22-23. Used by permission of Morehouse-Barlow Co., Inc., N. Y.

of intercessions for his people. Miss Slater adds this important testimony:

> Everyone who surveyed the life of Bishop Brent knew the source of its power. Even children knew. Sitting on the porch of the house of a friend one morning before breakfast, he was caught unaware by the children of the house, who had tiptoed out and in again. "Did you say good morning to the Bishop?" their mother asked. "No, mother," was their answer. "We could see by his face that he was praying, and we didn't like to disturb him." He knew the secret of "praying without ceasing" which is to pray sometimes with words—as often as the framework of a busy life allows—but also to pray with thoughts and energies, with hands and feet. He often wrote about this sort of prayer. It was central in his own character, prefaced activity, sanctified thought, surveyed and judged achievement. He strove to pray well that he might live well; but, equally, he strove to live well that he might pray well. His life moved both ways.*

As Brent's life unfolded, the passionate love which he had for our Lord manifested itself not only in the care of souls and in pastoral adventure for Christ, but also in his vision of the whole Church at one within itself. I remember his saying, "Christianity will not have run its full race until it has been through the mind of the Orient." The many facets of his extraordinary character came to their climax in his celebrated leadership of the Conference on Faith and Order at Lausanne in 1927, two years before his death.

---

* *Op. cit.*, pp. 70-71.

The impact of this life has not even yet made its fullest contribution. He still inspires the dreams of those in every branch of the Church who are today insisting that there shall be a practical, tenable result of Christ's prayer for unity. Those who share this vision and this hope, however, will do well to remember that the power which gave it rise in the case of Charles Brent was the daily and hourly life of prayer which enabled him so often to see as God sees and to act effectually both toward persons and toward the whole Church as God had appointed him.

1
PRAYERS FOR PERSONAL NEEDS

There are but two great realities in the vast universe —the heart of God and the heart of man, and each is ever seeking the other. It is this that makes adventure for God not an experiment, but a certainty. The appeal issuing from man's abysmal need is met by the amplitude of the divine supply.

The thought of God's keeping tryst with us is a winsome thought. When we go to pray, God has already come to the meeting place. We are never there first. He is indeed more ready to hear than we to pray, more ready to give more than we desire or deserve than we to ask. He comes not in the spirit of toleration but of ardent love. The great thing to remember is that God, being who He is, is more ready to hear than we to pray, more eager to give than we to receive, more active to find us than we to find Him. God is ever seeking man: His ear is more sensitive to the words, His heart to the desires, of men than the aspen leaf to the summer breeze, than the compass needle to the call of the poles.

Yes, prayer is speech Godward, and worship is man's whole life of friendship with God, the flowing out, as it were, of all that tide of emotion and service which is love's best speech.

On Waking

O heavenly Father, our Lover and Creator, in whom we live and move and have our being, at whose touch darkness gives place to light and night to day, lay Thy morning hand on all our faculties which sleep and fill them with the light of Thy life, that we may rejoice in the performance of the hard tasks which are the portion of strong men. (1)

O Light of the world, who daily enterest our conscious life on the wings of the dawn, illumine our minds this day with wisdom and our hearts with joy, that, being defended by the brightness of Thy countenance from the darkness of sin, we may radiate Thy gracious influence among our fellowmen to the purification of human life and the honor of Thy great name. (2)

O God, who hast folded back the black mantle of the night to clothe us in the golden glory of the day, chase from our hearts all gloomy thoughts and make us glad with the brightness of hope, that we may effectively aspire to unwon virtues; through Jesus Christ our Lord. (3)

Lord of the dawn, dispel the darkness of our hearts by the light of Thy truth as we reverently approach Thy glorious presence. Reveal to us day by day the path of eternal life, that with settled purpose and single mind we may pursue an unfaltering course until night falls and we are received into safe lodging with Thee who givest Thy beloved sleep. (4)

Lord, make me conscious of Thy holiness and majesty; teach me to know and to do Thy will; pour into my heart such love towards Thee, that, loving Thee above all things, I may obtain Thy gracious promises; through Jesus Christ our Lord. (5)

At the Break of Day

O God, whose name is Savior, deliver us this day, on the fair threshold of which we stand, from the enemies we fear and the sins we hate. Touch our hearts with the peace that passeth understanding and inspire our wills with that quiet courage that is never dismayed or daunted. Hear our prayers for the neglected, the burdened, the stained. Raise the fallen with Thy strong hand, heal the sick, care for the wounded, receive into blessed abodes the dying. Encompass with love our friends and foes, that by its fire misunderstandings may be burned away. Guide the Church, purify the nation, and save all mankind, O Blessed One, God and man. (6)

Heavenly Father, beneath whose sentinel vigilance we rest and labor, at the beginning of this fair day we thank Thee for Thy watchful protection through the hours of our unconsciousness. As Thou didst not fail us when in the night we lay still and babe-like in Thine arms but didst challenge and dispel the forces that threatened harm, so now, O Guardian of our waking hours, be light and might to us as we gird ourselves for our activities in the sunshine of this

26

hopeful, happy day. As Thou hast raised us pure from our beds, so send us forth splendid for our duty. Free us from morbid fancies, the tyrannous oppression of sins that refuse to be forgotten though long since forgiven, and all influences that will spoil or soil the effectiveness of our lives. Give us reality in thought, sincerity in utterance, modesty in expression, that self may die and make room for Thee to live. Make our duty a joy, our difficulties a tonic, our achievements a blessing to our fellows. Speed us on our day's journey, that we may reach the goal of Thy placing; and when night falls, fold us to Thy bosom and renew in us the life that flows from Thee to Thy children, so that sleeping and waking, resting and toiling, we may not be separated from Thee from whom we came, in whom we live, to whom we go. (7)

O God, creation's secret force, whose hand last night lit the fixed order of the starry heavens with the wild streamers of the North, we thank Thee that Thou didst share with us the mystic splendor of the sky beneath which afterwards we slept in the bosom of Thy love. Now as Thou sendest forth the dawn to perform its daily miracle of renewal in plain and forest and mountain, pour the light of pure wisdom and the fire of undaunted purpose into our lives, that, assured of Thine indwelling, we may fulfill our duty to God and man with the blitheness of the birds and the masterfulness of the storm. Teach us this day some new song of unselfish service; endue us with the inner beauty of simplicity that will radiate peace in the ways of men; crown us with hope that will brighten as the day wanes; and when night comes grant that it may not take us unawares or startle us with fears. Carry us through the sunset into the glory of the day that knows no night, and give us place in the firmament where the stars are made brighter by the strong shining of the Sun of Righteousness, Jesus Christ our Lord. (8)

The love of the Father enfold me; the wisdom of the Son enlighten me; the fire of the Holy Spirit inflame me. (9)

On Coming to God in Worship

Heavenly Father, who in the richness of Thy love invitest men into conscious fellowship with Thee, grant that we may find Thy mystic presence in the Church's solemn assembly where we gather to adore Thee in the wonder of Thy beauty, in the splendor of Thy truth, and in the joy of Thy loving-kindness revealed in Thy Son Jesus Christ our Lord. (10)

O God, the wonders of whose being rise above our minds in regal splendor, we bow in awed reverence before Thy divine majesty and worship Thee who art past understanding. Knowing Thee, not as Thou knowest us, but dimly as in a mirror, we thank Thee for the abundant self-showing of Thyself in the face of Jesus Christ. Let the clear flame of Thy love in our hearts so kindle in us responsive love that we may more and more know Thee as Thou art in all the brightness and beauty of Thy glory; through Jesus Christ our Lord. (11)

To Advance in Holiness and Peace

Father of all, controlling the visible order and guiding the hidden destiny of man, we approach Thee with love and awe and eager hope and thanksgiving. We love Thee because Thou first hast loved us and changed our heart of stone into a heart of flesh. We bow with wonder and reverence before the splendor of Thy divine life. We aspire to become like Thee, as true children of a heavenly Father. Therefore we pray Thee to manifest Thy life in our lives. Take from us all sordidness and meanness and hatred of our fellows. Help us to forgive as we are forgiven. Give us honor and truthfulness, purity and sweet temper, courage and gentleness. All that we ask for ourselves we ask for others, beseeching Thee to give not in accord with the feebleness and poverty of our petitions but from the inexhaustible wealth of Thy riches.

Bless our friends and relatives and keep them always in the arms of Thy love, protecting both souls and bodies from every evil and mischance. We offer Thee the gratitude of lives that have been richly blessed and favored, praying for strength to mold our thanksgiving into deep devotion and singleness of purpose, so that as we advance in years we may advance in piety and holiness and peace, hiding our lives more and more deeply in Thee with Christ who is our life until He manifests Himself in glory, that we also may be manifested with Him, to whom with the Father and the Spirit be all honor and glory forever. (12)

Invitation to the Holy Spirit

O God, who givest Thy Spirit without measure to those who prepare for Him a dwelling, make us worthy temples of His presence, that, our souls and bodies being swept clean of evil and adorned with virtue, we may joyfully welcome the heavenly guest in His full splendor to the sanctification of our lives; through Jesus Christ our Lord. (13)

Blessed Spirit of God, come to us in all Thy fullness and power, to clothe us in our nakedness, to enrich us in our poverty, to inflame us in our feebleness. Be closer to us than breathing, nearer than hands or feet. As lovers live each in each, so live in us and we in Thee. As the fire gives of itself to the molten iron, so give Thy presence to us. As the branches are in the vine, so may we abide in Thee. As birds mount upward through the air toward the sun, so may we ascend into Thy light and life. Enfold our bodies in Thy health. Compass our minds with Thy wisdom. Saturate our souls with Thy righteousness. Fire our wills with Thy might. Melt our hearts with Thy love. Do everything at all times to make us wholly Thine, until Thy wealth is ours and we are lost in Thee. (14)

At the Lord's Table

O Christ of the Eucharist, who in a special manner dost manifest Thyself to Thy people in the Sacrament of Thy Body and Blood, make Thyself known to us in the breaking of the Bread, that by faith we may clearly see Thy form and humbly adore Thy presence, who art God forever and ever. (15)

O Christ of the Passion, who at the Last Supper didst bequeath to the Church a perpetual memorial of the sacrifice of the Cross, help us in this holy sacrament steadfastly to contemplate Thy redeeming love, that we may ever be mindful of the price wherewith Thou hast bought us; who livest and reignest with the Father and the Holy Ghost, ever one God, world without end. (16)

Feed Us that We May Live

O Living Bread, that camest down from heaven to give abundant life to the world in this sacrament of the holy food, feed us with Thy body and the blood, that we may live in Thy life, labor in Thy strength, and inherit Thy joy; who livest and reignest God world without end. (17)

Fellow Guest at Thy Table

Grant, O Son of God, that as Thou and the Father art one, so we Thy people may be bound together in Thee. Unite in mutual forbearance, loyalty, and brotherly kindness, us Thy brethren who are fellow guests at this Thy table, that we, being moved by the common impulse of Thine eternal purpose, may promote the peace of Thy Kingdom in the daily interminglings of our common life; whom with the Father and the Holy Ghost we worship and glorify as God forever and ever. (18)

For True Repentance

I, Thy derelict, cry to Thee. Once I was a fair craft laden with the rich treasures of manhood, bound for Thy haven. Then came the storms of desire and shallows of pride, and all that remains is this bruised and battered derelict, useful only as Thou canst use fragments and wrecks, with hope of reaching final harbor only as Thou canst guide and save. (19)

O Savior, who in the completeness of Thy manhood art still Babe of Bethlehem and Child of Nazareth, restore in me the simplicity I have tampered with, the transparency I have obscured, the childlikeness I have lost, that the shattered fragments of my innocence may be assembled anew in the beauty of Thy sanctity; who with the Father and the Holy Ghost art God forever and ever. (20)

Eternal Father, who alone canst control the days that are gone and the deeds that are done, remove from my burdened memory the weight of past years, that being set free both from the glamor of complacency and the palsy of remorse, I may reach forth unto those things which are before and press toward the mark for the prize of the high calling of God in Christ Jesus. (21)

O Jesus, help me to be true to the dictates of conscience, through the agency of which the voice of God's will speaks to my life. Rid me of the disabling consequences of past sin. Make my penitence so complete that I may no longer be controlled by the evil past but that a life remolded from the past in imagination and power may pour its power into my present. Deliver me from the ambition to please others, and from whatever delicately toned selfishness debilitates my will. Let me never be a slave to the corrupt popular taste. Make my moral and spiritual character robust and positive that I may be a friend of Thy friends and a constructive force in my generation.

(22)

Repentance Which Is of Thy Will

Lord, give me the repentance which is of the will, that, not only in desire but also in intention and effort, I may embrace what is good, especially those virtues which once I neglected or refused, and so be endued with power to accept Thy pardon; through Jesus Christ our only Mediator and Advocate. (23)

O God, who requirest of me only such things as will turn to my profit, and who art pained by my least act of waywardness, warm my heart until it is aflame with love toward Thee, that my chief delight may be to bring Thee joy by my fidelity to Thy counsels; through Jesus Christ our Lord. (24)

High Aspiration

O God, can I ask more than that Thou shouldst be a father to me or that I should be a son to Thee? This is the height of heights. There is nothing beyond except that which already is here. There can be nothing tomorrow but that which is now—Thou the Father who art Love and Thou Love who art the Father. As Thou art to me, so be to all men. As I am so are they—sinners; as I am so are they—sinners beloved. But I would fain be not sinner beloved but saint beloved—holy because Thou art holy. As is the father, so must be the son. My Lord and God, I humbly aspire, I daringly aspire, to be as Thou art. Let Thy fatherly love set aflame in my heart filial love, brotherly love. Then, Father, let come what may, I shall have achieved in Thee and for Thee; to whom be ascribed all honor and glory and might and holiness through the ages of ages. (25)

Help me, O Captain of my salvation, to fight my way through the narrow lanes of self-discipline and up the steeps of virtue till I reach the summit of aspiration, where there is the pure air of freedom in the fortress of Thy love. (26)

To Hear the Music of Thy Counsels
O God, whose low, sweet song of love is never silent in the souls of men, make us skilled to hear the music of Thy counsels, that, vibrating with Thy message, we may learn to sing to Thee in tones of freedom and responsive joy, and so complete the antiphony that draws earth within the gates of heaven's choir; through Jesus Christ our Lord. (27)

O King of the ages, incorruptible, invisible, the only wise God, give me grace to look not at the things which are seen but at the things which are not seen, that enthralled by the broad splendor of the divine ideal and sustained by the freedom of a clean and sound conscience, I may lead men to embrace and rejoice in the faith once delivered to the saints; through Him to whom with Thee and the Spirit of God be honor and glory unto the ages of ages. (28)

O God, make me strong that I may use my strength as a shield wherewith to protect others, so that of them Thou givest me I may lose none; through Jesus Christ our Lord. (29)

Lord of love, with the whole world to love Thou dost not fail to love me. Give me to lean my full weight on Thee that losing myself in Thee I may have Thy life as my life. (30)

O Father, who hast unveiled what Thou art through the life and teaching of Jesus Christ, we too desire to be perfect even as Thou art perfect. Deliver us from all pettiness of spirit, and from the bondage of revenge, retaliation, and resentment. Teach us to love with a strong, serving love those who hate us, and to pray with burning desire for blessing on those who persecute us, that we may be worthy children of Thee, O Father, who makest the sun to rise on the evil and the good, and sendest rain on the just and the unjust. (31)

Light a Candle in Our Hearts

Lord, we are only what we are in Thy sight; unto Thee all hearts are open, from Thee no secrets are hid. Light a candle in our hearts that we may see what is therein and sweep out the rubbish from Thy dwelling place. We aspire to Thy beatitudes—humility and mournings, meekness and hunger and thirst after righteousness; mercy and purity of heart; peacemaking and persecution for righteousness' sake; that being clothed in heavenly garments we may rejoice in Thy salvation; through Jesus Christ our Lord. (32)

Heavenly Father, deliver us Thy children from the slavery of things and enlighten us with Thy Spirit that we may choose the glorious liberty of the sons of God, that looking not at the things which are seen but at the things which are unseen, we may claim Thy promises which exceed all that we can desire; through Jesus Christ our Lord. (33)

Lofty Ambition

Give us, Lord, lofty ambition such as will be satisfied with nothing less than the noble best and nothing short of the goal of final reality, that we may come to know the truth and that the truth may make us free; through Him who is the way, the truth, and the life, Jesus Christ. (34)

O Lord Jesus Christ, Head of the mystical body of which we are members, cleanse our eyes to see for Thee, quicken our ears to hear for Thee, open our lips to show forth Thy praise, give our hands skill to do what Thou biddest, make our feet swift to go whither Thou guidest, that Thy will may be done on earth as it is in heaven. (35)

Self-Dedication

O Father, I have been called by Harvard University to speak to Thy sons of the things that belong to their peace. But except Thou too call me my words will be uttered in vain and be but empty sound. Let me hear Thy voice bidding me serve the youth of this great center of opportunity, and make me responsive to Thy counsels that I may set forth the truth with force and ardor. Help me to fit my life more closely into Thine eternal purpose without reserve or self-will. Endow me with singleness of motive, strength of will, blamelessness of life, and devotion to Thee, that I being a true leader may inspire my fellows to rise to the full height of their responsibilities as leaders of men; through Jesus Christ our Lord. (36)

O God, who hast fathomed human life by living it and forever holding in Thy divine nature the fullness of experience garnered upon earth, I believe that Thou wilt give me courage and steadfastness when the lights grow dim and the gloom falls. Help me in the high noon of my career to draw strength from sources that cannot be drained or diminished by the fevered lips of adversity, so that when sorrows assail I may not flinch, when failure wraps my activities in unyielding folds I may not despair, when evil tidings cloud my sky my heart may stand fast and be not afraid. Fight in me, my God, as Thou hast fought for me, till the task is done, the battle fought, the experience gained, and I am admitted into the company of those who are Thy friends forever. (37)

To Humbly Live in Thee

O God, who hast not yet rejected the unworthy and flickering flame of my service, fix my purpose in Thine own Self from whom it came, that being fed by Thee, who art the Source of all light, I may not fail to hold aloft the torch of Thy glory by humbly living in Thee and for Thee; through Jesus Christ our Lord. (38)

O God, open my eyes to see, cleanse my life to do, nerve my courage to bear all that Thy will wills for me. Grant me to love, to rejoice, to be tranquil, to be pure, to be true, to trust, so that before I go hence and be no more seen I may be known by Thee as a loyal and loving bond servant of Thine and of those who are Thine. (39)

I know, my Master, that in giving myself anew as I now do, I give myself to peace that abides serene in tribulation and to security that stands firm in peril. I renew my allegiance to the best I know, believing that Thou wilt lead me into a higher best which Thou hast in keeping for Thy friends and followers, among whom I desire to be numbered; through Jesus Christ our Lord. (40)

Grant, O heavenly Father, that we may know ourselves to be Thy children, dependent upon Thee for wisdom and goodness. Give us faith to seek Thy will and strength to do it, that rejoicing in the glorious liberty of the children of God we may have Thy peace all our days and do the work for which Thou hast sent us; through Jesus Christ our Lord. (41)

Be My King

Lord Jesus, I accept Thee as my King. Take me as Thy subject and rule my unruly life. Thy reign is just and generous. Unveil its beauty to me. Thou didst win Thy throne by conquest, and wouldst share it with all who conquer self. Make it my joy to do Thy will, whatever it may be. Help me to find satisfaction in thwarting my self-indulgent desires, that I may promote the Kingdom which is not of this world. (42)

Lord Jesus, be my King and rule me within and without. Govern my mind, shape my motives, control my desires. Share with me Thy crucified life that everything wicked and weak may die from my nature. Give me the will to suffer that I may have the power that is born only from the womb of pain. And grant that dying with Thee in Thy death I may rise to life eternal. (43)

For Self-Control

Grant, merciful Lord, that I may so strive as to win such mastery of self as will lay at Thy disposal for Thy purposes my whole being. Teach me to be temperate from day to day. Nerve me to pluck out my right eye or to cut off my right hand if by being maimed I may become more nearly whole. Give me the enthusiasm of self-sacrifice that will find interest in experimenting in difficult things for Thy Kingdom's sake. Through the avenues of self-discipline pour Thy healing streams till my wounds, becoming witnesses of Thy compassion and power and no longer a reproach to my manhood and solemn vows, are turned into glorified scars. The more desperate my case the more insistently I claim of Thee complete renewal and unbounded self-mastery in body and soul; for Thou art a full fountain and hast all power in heaven and earth, to whom be all honor and majesty and dominion forever and ever. (44)

Endue us, O God, with such a measure of patience as will enable us to win our lives, that we may never, "even for one moving moment, lose that complete possession of ourselves which is the first condition of good service." (45)

Control of Our Minds

Help us, heavenly Father, so to gain control of our minds that we may always direct our thoughts to do Thy bidding, and that whatsoever things are just, whatsoever things are pure, whatsoever things are lovely, whatsoever things are of good report, if there be any virtue and if there be any praise, we may think on these things. (46)

Lord, lift us into the uplands of righteous and just living. Inspire us with a vision of the splendor and the freedom of self-control, that we may gain that inner poise and calm which is the source of our greatest social power. Clothe our souls with a purity that consumes all uncleanness of thought as with a raging flame. Make us accurate and truthful within that we may think the truth and that the truth may make us free; through Jesus Christ our Savior. (47)

Give Me Thy Help

Lord, give me Thy help not only to speak the truth in love but also to live it with power. Plant in my heart the seed of sincerity, that I may never palter. Make me steadfast and sure, come what may, that being allied to Thee and Thy purpose I may share in the light of Thy life and mount upward with glad and tireless step until I shall have attained even as Christ attained; through the same Christ, our Master and Guide. (48)

O Author and Giver of Life, who rejoicest to make the desert like a garden of the Lord and the wilderness to blossom as a rose, fertilize with the breath of Thy mouth the barren portions of my nature, that, instead of the thorn of _____ may come up the fig tree of _____, and instead of the brier of _____ may come up the myrtle tree of _____. Let there be showers of blessing until the blossoms of promise come to full fruition in the attainment of those virtues of which I am destitute. Grant this, O Holy Spirit, who with the Father and Son art worshiped and glorified as God forever and ever. (49)

Thou, O Lord God, ever rejoicest in supreme bliss and Thou wouldst make that which is Thine our own; nor dost Thou wait for us to merit Thy gifts before their bestowal. Wherefore, Lord, relying on Thy kindness, I pray Thee for such inner brightness as I am able to receive and Thou to give. And if gloom and shadows envelop my life, engulf them and me in Thy bliss that I may not be overwhelmed by despair or separated from Thee in whose light alone can I see light. (50)

Give me, O Lord, love that embraces all, sympathy that always understands, patience that never flags, loyalty that cannot play false. Stiffen my will, that it may choose the right way even when it is the hard way. Liberate me from the tyranny of evil, that neither persons nor things may vitiate my judgment or enslave my purpose. Thou who art the best, mold me after the pattern of Thyself until I am Thy friend and the friend of Thy friends, even as Thou art my friend and Friend of my friends. (51)

Give me, my Master, the gift of simplicity that sees with a clear eye and acts with a firm hand. Enable me to be just toward those who are unjust to me. Release me from the sins of indirection and vacillation, and teach me the ways of directness and stability. (52)

Lord Jesus, behold me Thy poor, half-hearted disciple who comes to Thee frequently by night and for lack of courage screens his best emotions and stifles his highest aspirations, and let the spectacle of Thy self-offering move me to boldness. Banish silly fear from my life—fear of criticism, of opposition, or ridicule. Entwine the strands of my life in the web of Thy purpose so that through fellowship with Thy sufferings I may attain to the glory of Thy Resurrection.

(53)

O Jesus, who didst destroy the strongholds of evil by penetrating into their heart and exposing their impotency to harm or imprison human life, deliver me from fear by guiding me into the secret chambers of the forces that are arrayed against righteousness, that the strong man may be bound and the spoils of his house added to the wealth of Thy Kingdom.

(54)

O God, who art the sure foundation of life, deliver me from the fickleness of my nature which bends before temptation as the reed before the tempest. Love alone can make me loyal. Bind my life to Thine in unbreakable unity. Help me to look to Thee in hard moments and find the strength that I lack. Keep my heart faithful and my lips truthful that I may never deny Thee or betray my brethren. (55)

Lord, teach us to pray so that our lives may mingle with Thine in intimate communion and fellowship. Grant us a zeal to work with Thee, to cooperate in Thy purpose for our lives. Enable us to forgive even as we have been forgiven, that in serving Thee and in service to our fellowmen we may fulfill Thy ambitions for us. (56)

To Benefit by Thy Chastisements

O God, teach us to benefit by Thy chastisements. Keep in our remembrance the certain issue of a sinful life, lest, forgetting Thy holiness, we may suffer Thy whole displeasure. (57)

An Inspired Day

O Word of God, who givest our thoughts that we may speak them back to Thee, I offer Thee the first fruits of my heart and mind, beseeching Thee to heed my loftiest aspirations, and to grant that as they have come from Thee as promptings, so they may return to Thee as righteous deeds, carrying on high my will made captive to Thy wisdom, who livest and reignest forever and ever. (58)

O God, who callest men for the good of Thy Kingdom to forego the completeness and joys of wedded life, preserve me this day in continence and glowing chastity, that, passing triumphantly through temptation, I may at last be clothed in white raiment and follow the Lamb whithersoever He goeth, who liveth and reigneth with Thee and the Holy Ghost one God forever and ever. (59)

Draw our affections, Lord, up to the heights where Thou dwellest, that, our hearts being set not on things seen but on things unseen, our lives may be shaped according to Thy pattern and filled with the vision of Thy beauty. (60)

The Daily Walk

O Christ, our Brother, who in this very flesh hast reached the land where joy and service are one, lead us thither, that where Thou art there we may also be. Teach us heirs of mortality how to practice immortality in our daily walk, that in the midst of death we may ever be in life. Help us to claim as present wealth the glorious things to be, the battles won and tasks complete, that we may rejoice in hope and by faith give substance to the glory of the unseen. (61)

O God, who orderest the common things of the common day, dignify by Thy presence and aid the trivial round and routine tasks of Thy servant whose hope is in Thee, that least duties may be grandly done and all activities marked with the seal of Thy righteousness; through Jesus Christ our Lord. (62)

The Day's Work and Duties

O God, who knowest human life by having lived it, reveal to us its deep meanings, its scope, its power, its beauty. Help us to give first place not to the things which are seen but to the things which are not seen. Make us sensitive to the voice of conscience, that we may be honorable, high-minded, and courageous.

Conduct us into that vast liberty which is the heritage of the sons of God. As Thou didst care for us sleeping, guard us waking. Be with us in our tasks and pleasures this day. Deliver us from gnawing anxiety by that trust that sees all things working for good to those that love Thee. Behold the great world of men, Thy world—our relations, friends, and acquaintances everywhere. Bind us together in the unity of the Spirit and the bond of peace, and grant that justice may reign in our nation. Finally, we pray for compassion on the neglected, the weary, the sorrowing, the sick, the wounded, the dying. Give rest and peace to the dead and bring us all into Thine eternal Kingdom.

(63)

Clothe our weak timidity with Thine own unwavering courage, good Lord, that we, fearing nothing and daring all things, may spend our full strength on the day's duty to the dismay of the enemy and the establishment of Thy Kingdom; through Christ our Savior. (64)

The Battle of Life

O God, who hast proclaimed the victorious destiny of man by Thyself achieving it in human form, give us the will to win the battle of life, that we may find strength in weakness, quiet in turbulence, and triumph in failure; through Jesus Christ our Lord. (65)

O Captain of my life, who never failest to lead Thy loyal soldiers to victory, fill my soul with the joy of battle, that I may fear nothing but cowardice and, in the power of Thy comradeship, may speed with unwavering feet toward the day of final triumph, when night will turn into day, sorrow into joy, and death into the abundance of Thy Kingdom. (66)

In Hours of Hardship

Grant, O Lord, as Thou hast cast my lot in a fair ground, that I may show forth contentment by rejoicing in the privileges with which Thou hast strewn my path, and by using to the full my opportunities for service. In hours of hardship, preserve me from self-pity and endow me with the warrior's mind, that even in the heat of battle I may be inspired with the sense of vocation and win the peace of the victor; through Jesus Christ our Lord. (67)

O King, whose Kingdom is in this world and not of it, give to us the spirit of absolute loyalty to Thee that we may not fight with the weapons of force or guile, partisanship or rivalry. Cleanse Thy Church, which is an agent of Thy Kingdom, from the sins of separation and theory. Give us faith that declares itself in life, hope that maketh not ashamed, and love as wide as the world of men. (68)

Be very near to us, Lord, in the abundance of Thy life, that Thy wisdom may be our guiding light, Thy righteousness the goal of our effort, Thy strength the armor of our warfare; through Jesus Christ our Lord. (69)

Comrades in Christian Service

Lord Jesus, who didst stretch out Thine arms of love on the hard wood of the Cross, that all men might come within the reach of Thy saving embrace, clothe

us in Thy spirit that we, stretching forth our hands
in loving labor for others, may bring those who know
Thee not to the knowledge and love of Thee, who
with the Father and the Holy Ghost livest and reignest
one God. (70)

Valiant Lord, who in our very nature didst fight to
win and labor to achieve, clothe us with Thy valor,
that we of Thy household, being delivered from the
fear of living as Christians, may unite as comrades
in service to attack the problems of our troubled day,
with serene mind and victorious will, till our last foe
is vanquished and our last task finished to Thy honor
and glory, who livest and reignest God forevermore.
(71)

To Live Christianly
Grant us, Lord, the will to live Christianly, that by
Thy might we may storm the fortress of evil and set
free its prisoners into the glorious liberty of the children of God. (72)

Atmosphere of Brotherhood
Lord, lift us out of private mindedness and give us
public souls to work for Thy Kingdom, by daily creating that atmosphere of brotherhood by a happy
temper, a friendly mind, and a generous heart, which
alone can bring in the great Peace to Thy honor and
the comfort of mankind. (73)

O God, source of all wisdom, unite us in a common purpose to seek and to know the truth as revealed in Christ, that, companying with one another in our pilgrimage Godward, we may together attain that perfect knowledge of Thee in which standeth our eternal life; through Jesus Christ our Lord. (74)

In a Time of Decision

O God of missionaries, who, seven years since, didst guide my reluctant, halting steps into the unknown vastness of the great Orient, that I might bear witness to Thy truth, I thank Thee for having used my stained and timid life to this end. Before Thee I lament my ofttimes deficiency and those long-indulged weaknesses that have once and again betrayed me into sin, imploring Thee to block their progress, that they bring no shame to Thy Church nor work hurt to Thy children. Gather into Thy skillful and all-availing hands the slender thread of my achievements, and weave it into the fabric of Thy beneficent purposes.

Abundantly bless my dear fellow workers, who so fearlessly in response to my leadership have bent their endeavors to enlighten the ignorant, to relieve the distressed, and to succor the needy. If it be Thy will that I should continue to live and labor in the Philippine Islands, give me deepened humility, sunny contentment, and quickened zeal, that I may recompense the loyalty of my comrades by sympathetic considerateness and devotion to their interests. But if Thou wouldst have me lay down my task yonder, send them one more worthy and more wise than I, that the foundations that have been laid may be strengthened and the walls of Thy spiritual temple rise heavenward in power and beauty. (75)

O Spirit of God, Presider in the councils of the Church, who hast a second time moved the Diocese of _____ to call me, the least worthy of leaders, to become the successor of Thy saint, _____, fail not to be with and in me lest I answer amiss. It was beyond peradventure Thou who didst bid me first decline. I thank Thee that Thou didst through the days of seeking and waiting preserve my motive pure and my purpose noble. Now, O Lord of wisdom, be my guide again as I face the problem anew. Burn away with Thy most searching and pitiless flame the last shreds of self-will that may adhere to my judgment. Let me not fall victim to preference or to the lesser good. Let me rather tower in my decision, that whether I go or stay I may command conditions and not be their slave. Grant my petition, O Lord, that Thy truth may be magnified among men, and Thy Kingdom made glad. (76)

O Spirit of God, who, according to the Savior's promise, hast given me a right judgment in the perplexity of these past days, enable me to rejoice in Thy holy comfort. Let not the disappointment of friends or the misunderstanding of the world disturb my peace or weaken my sense of vocation. Fire me with new courage, that I may fight a good fight and keep the faith through the power of Thine unfailing presence; through Jesus Christ our Lord. (77)

In Time of Illness

Lord Jesus, at whose touch the unclean are cleansed
and the distressed made whole, let health reign in all
my members, that, the cause of sickness being dispelled
by Thy presence, my body may become a shrine
worthy of Thine indwelling and an instrument fitted
for Thy use, O great Physician and Lover of men.

(78)

Lord Jesus, who in the days of Thine earthly career
didst gather into the life of God the fullness of human
pain as a fact of experience, in order that Thou
mightest flood the life of man with divine health, remember now in Thy triumphant might Thy former
woes, and sustain in Thy compassionate and healing
arms my suffering body. Banish my depression and
fears by the cheering gladness of Thine unfailing sympathy, and encircle me with the soothing folds of Thy
victorious wholeness, giving me faith sufficient to
drink deep draughts from the invisible but abundant
springs of peace and strength, which are closer to me
than breathing, nearer than hands or feet; that I may
not die but live and declare the works of the Lord.

(79)

O Spirit of God, who art the life of men, destroy in
us the seeds of disease and death, that we may minister to our suffering fellows with healthy minds and
sound bodies. Out of the abundance of Thy brightness
dispel our shadows; with the fullness of Thy joys
outweigh our sorrows; in the wealth of Thy providence bury our anxieties, that we may add to our skill

those divine influences that further the work of healing and make us true servants and handmaidens of the great Physician, Jesus Christ our Lord. (80)

O God, I open my body to Thee and Thy Spirit that it may become Thy veritable temple where Thou wilt rejoice to dwell. Give me a body as clean and wholesome as that of a little child and as strong as that of a strong man. Teach me to use Thy power-become-mine in firm self-control that all my senses may be at Thy command. Touch with ordering and cleansing hand those functions that have been disarranged or befouled by reckless or evil use. Then send me, O Lord, to do those great tasks for others which strong hands and stout hearts alone can do; through Him who was dead and is alive forevermore and who holds the keys of Hades and death. (81)

Gratitude for Restored Health

We offer Thee our gratitude, heavenly Father, because Thou hast heard our prayers and restored to me, Thy servant, that measure of health and vigor which enables me to pursue my course on earth. Renew my devotion, clarify my vision, sustain my hands, that Thou mayest be justified in Thy dealing with me to the honor and glory of Thy great name; through Jesus Christ our Lord. (82)

Note: See also Section 4, "Prayers from His Diary," the entries for 24 September 1923 and 9 September 1925.

At Day's End

O most high, almighty, good Lord God, to Thee belong praise, honor, glory, and all blessing. Praised be our Lord God with all His creatures, and especially our brother the sun, who brings us the day, and who brings us the light; fair is he and shines with very great splendor; O Lord, he signifies to us Thee! Praised be our Lord for our sister the moon, and for the stars, which He hath set clear and lovely in heaven! Praised be our Lord for our brother the wind, and for air and cloud, calms and all weather by which Thou upholdest life in all creatures. Praised be our Lord for our sister water, who is very serviceable unto us and humble and precious and clean. Now that we have come to the hour of rest of our brother the sun, give us, too, rest in Thee. Fold our consciences in heavenly peace. Lift from our hands our tasks and all through the night bear in Thy bosom the full weight of our burdens and sorrows, that in untroubled slumber we may press our weakness close to Thy strength and win new powers for the morrow's duty from Thee who givest Thy beloved sleep. Be with those who watch and serve under the silent stars while we slumber; lighten their darkness, we beseech Thee, O Lord, and by Thy great mercy defend them from all perils and dangers of the night, and when the morning breaks, the morning of unclouded triumph and joy, give us and them a place in Thy Kingdom where Thou art the only and sufficient light; through Jesus Christ our Lord. (83)

O Lord Jesus Christ, who in the old days didst call Thy companions apart to find rest and refreshment in Thee, be with us now in this evening hour as we draw nigh to Thy side. Make us conscious of Thy nearness. Share with us Thy life—the whiteness of Thy purity, the comfort of Thy strength, the wonder of Thine eternal purpose. Lead us, day by day, deeper into the mystery of life, and make us interpreters of life to our fellowmen that we and they may obtain Thy promises. (84)

Evening Prayer During Pestilence

O almighty and most high God, our hope and our stronghold, in whom we trust, defend us under Thy wings that we may not be afraid for any terror by night nor for the pestilence that walketh in darkness. Give Thine angels charge over us to keep us in all our ways. With long life satisfy us and show us Thy salvation; through Jesus Christ our Lord. (85)

Evening Thanksgiving

Father of lights, from whose unshadowed home comes every good and perfect gift, I receive as from Thy hand my share in the common blessings which, without respect of persons, hourly descend upon mankind. I thank Thee for the special tokens of Thy friendship and personal care that have made me glad this day. Help me to use these and all Thy bounties according to Thy design, that my whole life may be a hymn of praise to Thee; through Jesus Christ our Lord. (86)

For mercies and blessings unknown and unnumbered we praise Thee, O God, beseeching Thee for grace to show our gratefulness in lives aflame with the desire and purpose to do Thy will and promote the interests of our King Jesus Christ, who with the Father and the Holy Spirit reigneth God world without end.

(87)

A Restful Night

O God, who hast drawn over weary day the restful veil of night, wrap our consciences in heavenly peace. Lift from our hands our tasks, and all through the night bear in Thy bosom the full weight of our burdens and sorrows, that in untroubled slumber we may press our weakness close to Thy strength and win new power for the morrow's duty from Thee who givest Thy beloved sleep. (88)

O God, who wast the brightness of the dawn's first rays and of the noontide's glory, according to Thy most sure promise fail not to give us light at evening time. Dispel by Thy pardoning love the gloom of this day's guilt, and through the hours of darkness keep bright in our souls the star of trust in Thy sheltering care; through Jesus Christ our Lord. (89)

Near the End of Life

Thou, Father, didst light the star of my life at Thine own lamp of light and love. For Thy sleepless care each day from dawn to dark and through the silent hours of the night, I thank Thee. For family ties, for dear ones loved long since and lost awhile, for loyal friends and comrades true, I praise Thee. For joys that never die, for perils past, for sins forgiven, I glorify Thee. For the will to serve, the power to do, the strength to bear, I pray Thee. When the shadows fall and evening comes, give me grace to die peacefully, victoriously. When I enter into Thy nearer presence, receive me compassionately, lovingly. (90)

O God of man, who hast brought us through the difficulties and dangers of life, be with us yet until we die. We have done wrong and need Thy forgiveness. Make us clean where we are stained, and strong where we are weak. Help us to lay hold of our various tasks with willing hands and cheerful faces, and to do them with thoroughness. Inspire us with respect for ourselves and for one another, that we may be worthy of Thy regard. (91)

At Life's End

O God, whose guiding hand has until now led me safely through the changes of this world, be with me at the close of my work as Thou wast with me at the beginning. Though my faith has been feeble and my efforts faint, Thou hast never failed me. Abide with me as the day wanes and give me a resting-place near Thy feet when the night falls; through Him who turns sorrow into joy and darkness into light, Jesus Christ our Lord. (92)

In the Hour of Our Departure

O Thou who holdest in life Thy servants when their feet tread the valley of the shadow of death, be with us now and in the hour of our departure, that with Thy faithful people whose course on earth is finished, especially _____, we may be delivered from the power of the enemy, cleansed from all our sins, and admitted into Thy heavenly Kingdom; through Jesus Christ our Lord. (93)

2

PRAYERS FOR PERSONS, OCCASIONS, AND CAUSES

Noontide is intercession time—not exclusively but fittingly. At that moment Christ entered into the most mysterious and unfathomable recesses of the Atonement. It is a natural resting spot, too, from the business of life, wherein we may exchange outer for inner activities, disciplining self-interest by praying for others and their interests.

———— • ————

Intercessory prayer is not a work of extraordinary merit but a necessary element of devotion. It is the simple recognition in worship of the fundamental law of human life that no man lives or dies alone. But intercession rises to sublime heights when it claims the privilege and the power for each child of God to gather up in his arms the whole family to which he belongs, and carry it with its multifold needs and its glorious possibilities into the presence of the common Father for blessing and protection. It is grand to feel that the Christian can lift, by the power of prayer, a myriad as easily as one, that he can hold in his grasp the whole Church as firmly as a single parish, and can bring down showers of blessing on an entire race as readily as the few drops needed for his own little plot.

There is no more delicate service in the whole round of human action than that of intercessory prayer. It is so hidden as to have a special beauty on that account. While men are all unconscious that we are thinking of them, we fold our arms about them and bring them up before God for blessing and guidance. Intercessory prayer might be defined as loving our neighbor on our knees.

———•·•———

Intercession is the soul of service. It gives spiritual meaning to that which we do for others; it makes plain to us just how and where we can best help our fellows; and it furnishes us with a sympathy for and an insight into human life that can be produced through no other channel. It may end in making us poor in pocket, in sending us on some hazardous errand to the needy, or in creating the spirit of adventure for God that will lift us into the uttermost parts of the earth. But its compensation is the bestowal upon its user of an enriched manhood and a tender heart. What spiritual and hidden agencies are let loose by intercession upon those who are prayed for it is hard to determine; but we know, without understanding how or why, that powerful influences for good are released by this ennobling devotion which agitates with new effectiveness the unresting hands of God.

For the Family

Shed the bright rays of Thy light, O Father, upon this
family and household, that every member of the
same, made confident by Thy guidance, may fulfil
his daily duty with pure motive and gallant heart.
Be close to us in times of stress and strain, that our
courage and our hope may never fail. Let Thy sheltering arm protect us, that we may be valiant in all peril.
Turn Thou for us sorrow into joy, darkness into sunshine, death into life, so that when evening comes and
our work on earth is done we may pass triumphantly
into the uplands of fellowship in Thy family above;
through Jesus Christ our Lord. (94)

For Our Nearest and Dearest

Deliver us from meanness and selfishness. Give us the
heart to be kind to one another, not tempting to evil
but ready to lend a helping hand to the tempted, the
weak and the discouraged. We pray Thee for those we
love at home—our relatives and friends and all who
are bound to us by ties of kinship or affection. Keep
them in life and honor, and grant that we may never
have cause to be ashamed of them or they of us. Support us all through life's journey and bring us safely
to the land of light and love where Thou art King.
(95)

Father, grant to my dear ones all the best gifts Thou
hast ever bestowed on me, and, adding bounty to
bounty, enlarge Thy favor so as to flood their lives
with treasures and blessings beyond my understanding

to know or my merits to receive; through Him who, being rich, became poor that we through His poverty might become rich, even Thy Son Jesus Christ our Lord. (96)

O God, fulfil every need of theirs according to Thy riches in glory in Christ Jesus, and the peace of God which passeth all understanding guard their hearts and thoughts in Jesus Christ. (97)

For Loved Ones Departed

O King of Paradise, where light abounds and life reigns, give to our dear ones who are with Thee, especially _____, a full share of Thy treasures, that they may always be white with Thy purity, tranquil with Thy peace, and glad with Thy joy. Let us live vividly in their present love as they live in ours, until the time of separation is past, and we are taken to the place whither they have gone before, there to dwell with them in the perfect fellowship that knows no end. (98)

For All Who Mourn

In Thy boundless compassion, O Lord, console all who mourn. Give to them that faith which sees in death but the gate to life eternal, so that with quietude and fearlessness they may continue their course on earth until by Thy call they are united to their loved ones gone before; through Jesus Christ our Lord. (99)

O God, let the hand of blessing rest upon Thy servant. Keep *him* ever constant in the integrity of faith and righteousness. Touch with consoling hand *his* sorrow. Give *him* tranquil wisdom in *his* responsibilities. Accompany *him* down life's pathway and enable *him* to ascend on high in heart and mind and with Thee continually dwell; through Jesus Christ our Lord. (100)

For Friends and Comrades

O God, who hast made pleasant and lovely the bonds of friendship, I thank Thee for the many friends and comrades with whom Thou hast enriched my life _____. Tighten the cords of love which unite us in Thee, and in death divide us not; through Jesus Christ our Lord. (101)

For Those Who Have Done Me Good

O Lord Jesus, who knowest them that are Thine when Thou rewardest Thy servants the prophets, remember, I beseech Thee, for good those who have taught me, rebuked me, counselled me, guided me: and in that day show them mercy. When Thou rewardest the saints, remember, I beseech Thee, for good those who have surrounded me with holy influences, borne with me, forgiven me, sacrificed themselves for me, loved me: and in that day show them mercy. When Thou regardest the great that fear Thy name, remember, I beseech Thee, for good those who have been my patterns of any virtue or grace, of repentance, acknowledgment of offences, begging of pardon, obedience, patience, perseverance: and in that day show them mercy. When Thou rewardest the small that fear Thy name, remember, I beseech Thee, for good ignorant disciples, halting followers, weak cross-bearers, the kneelers on feeble knees, the faint believers who faint not utterly: and in that day show them mercy. Nor forget any, nor forget me: but in that day show us mercy. (102)

For Benefactors

Be pleased, O Lord, to remember all those, our friends, whose gifts have enriched us. Do Thou good to them, and return all their kindness double into their own bosom, rewarding them with blessings, and sanctifying them with Thy graces, and bringing them to glory; through Jesus Christ our Lord. (103)

O Light of the world, whose name is the Orient, cast Thy bright beams upon Thy servants _____ and all who by their prayers and gifts have brought Thee to Thine own in the isles of the Eastern Sea; and guide their feet into the way of peace, Thou Dayspring from on high who with the Father and the Holy Ghost art God world without end. (104)

For the Donor of the Cathedral

Look down from heaven, O Lord, and behold from the habitation of Thy holiness and glory Thy servant _____ who has conceived the desire to build a temple for Thy special presence among the sons of

65

men. Come unto her and make Thine abode with her, that she may rejoice in Thy comfort on earth and after this life be received into the house of many mansions on high; through Jesus Christ our Lord. (105)

For———and Other Stewards of Wealth

O God, the source and bestower of riches, behold with Thy favor _____ and all stewards of wealth. Deliver them from the love of money; crown them with the spirit of generosity; and lead them so to administer their trust as to rejoice in freedom, to relieve distress, and to promote the welfare of the Kingdom of God; through Jesus Christ our Lord. (106)

For Primitive Peoples

O wise and holy God, give us wisdom that we may understand these simple people among whom we live and labor. Enable us to draw them toward us by sympathy and bind them to us with the bands of confidence and affection. Give us mutual understanding of one another, that we may live in hallowed brotherhood, the strong bearing the burdens of the weak, and the weak enlarging their capacity by using to the utmost the gifts that they have. Teach us who are tangled in the web of complexity the value of simplicity as we view the contented, unembarrassed lives of the Igorots. And preserve the primitive peoples who are our wards from the evils and distractions of our civilization. Promote and advance the dispensation of the Spirit throughout the wild tribes of this archipelago; through Jesus Christ our Savior. (107)

For All Men Everywhere

O God, who willest all men to be saved and to come to the knowledge of the truth, hear the prayers that we offer for all men everywhere, for the mighty populous natives of historic fame, for the weak and timid tribes that have their retreat in the seclusion of the forest and the vastness of the great mountains. Give us conviction of worldwide mission. Select from our midst preachers and apostles who will proclaim Thy love in faith and truth, with wisdom and patience, to the breaking down the barriers of evil throughout the world and the enlightenment and peace of all mankind; through our only Mediator who gave His life a ransom for all, the Man Christ Jesus. (108)

For Pardon for My Flock

O Lord, the great and dreadful God, keeping the mercy and covenant to them that love Him, and to them that keep His commandments, we have sinned and committed iniquity, and have done wickedly, and have rebelled, even by departing from Thy precepts and from Thy judgments. O Lord, righteousness belongeth to Thee, but unto us confusion of face, as at this day. Behold us this night and heal all our infirmities. O Lord, according to Thy righteousness, I beseech Thee, let Thine anger and Thy fury be turned away from Thy people. O Lord, hear; O Lord, forgive; O Lord, hearken and do; defer not for Thine own sake, O my God, for we are Thy people and are called by Thy name. (109)

For Children

O Lord Jesus, who in the old days didst fold loving arms about the little ones that nestled to Thy bosom, and who in blessing them didst bring benediction to Thine own Self, wrap close the folds of Thine unsoiled innocency around the children of this generation, guarding their imaginations from unholy suggestions, their wills from debilitating influences, their bodies from defiling associations. Make me in motive and purpose as a little child, that when my life touches theirs, in blessing them I too may be blessed by their whiteness, and, with my hand in theirs, be allowed to enter into the wonders of the Kingdom of Heaven where Thou livest and reignest the childlike King of the children of God. (110)

Look with favor, heavenly Father, on little children everywhere. Defend them from the unkindness of men and all evil influences. Make us like to them that with them we may enter the Kingdom of Heaven; through Jesus Christ our Lord. (111)

For the Settlement and Orphanage of the Holy Child, Sagada, P. I.

Lord Jesus, let the memory of Thy childhood days move Thee to abide with us who dwell in the House of the Holy Child. Advance us in wisdom and stature, and in favor with God and men. Keep our hearts simple, our souls clean, and our hands industrious, that, following in Thy holy footsteps, we may at last reach Thy heavenly home, where Thou forever reignest the childlike King of the children of men. (112)

For Use of Boys of the House of the Holy Child

O Branch of David, make my boyhood straight and strong, that, bringing forth the fruit of the Spirit, I may become the protector of the weak, the champion of the good, and the beloved of the Lord, who livest and reignest God forever and ever. (113)

For Use of Girls of the House of the Holy Child

O holy God, who hast robed me in the lily white of maidenhood, wash me daily in the dew of Thy blessing and bathe me in the sunshine of Thy favor, that I may shed abroad the fragrance of a blameless life; through Jesus Christ our Lord. (114)

For Little Children Who Have Given Me Their Love

Blessed be Thy name, O God, for infants, the delight of the world. Reward the trustful love wherewith they love us with a double portion of Thy love. Bid men and angels guard them from aught that will soil their beauty or harm their fragrance. Grant that they may flourish like pure lilies in the courts of Thy house, imparting the whiteness of their innocence to us Thy servants who having stained our robes seek anew to become as little children: for of such is the Kingdom of Heaven. (115)

For Children by Those Who Would Become as Children

We thank Thee, heavenly Father, for the precious gift of children, the joy of our life and the hope of the world.

We thank Thee for Thy sympathy with and love for the little ones of every age, declared in the victorious entrance into human experience of Thy divine Son, Jesus Christ.

We praise Thee for the Babe of Bethlehem, the Boy of Nazareth, perfection and pattern of childhood, in whom heaven and earth blend.

We thank Thee for the trust committed to us to teach and train little children who alone have a clear title to the Kingdom of Heaven.

Heavenly Father, we pray Thee for all the little ones of our day, whether in our own land or in the farthest shores of the earth.

Gather into the arms of Thy tender compassion the lambs of Thy flock who are hungry and sick and forgotten and dying.

Defend from the perils of prosperity and ease those who thrive and live in pleasant places.

Upon us who are at this time gathered to further Thy Kingdom among children, bestow childlikeness and singleness of heart, without which we ourselves cannot know Thee or so much as see Thy Kingdom.

We pray Thee for sincerity of purpose, wisdom of mind, and modesty of expression in all our deliberations.

Bless our Sunday schools and multiply our opportunities until Thy truth is daily proclaimed and taught from day to day in all places of learning throughout our land.

Give to teachers integrity of character and an understanding of the truth as declared in Jesus Christ.

To the scholars grant a desire to know and to do Thy will, that they may become Thy beloved children in whom Thou art well pleased.

We present this our thanksgiving and prayer to Thee, O Father, for the honor of Thy great name, the advancement of Thy Kingdom, and the enduring benefit of our fellowmen, through Jesus Christ, the children's supreme Master and Teacher and ours. (116)

For a Children's Corner in a Parish Church

Grant Thy blessing, Lord, to this place where little children whom Thou dost love are wont to gather to talk with Thee. Be present in Thy love and favor with all who kneel here. Make Thyself known to them. Hear their prayers and make them true followers of Thine; through Jesus Christ our Lord. (117)

For Young People

Father, we praise Thee for the young, for those about to live. Give them souls of flame to search Thy counsels, and wills of steel to do Thy will. Make them honest workmen that they may work diligently while it is day. Refine their taste and correct their manners, that their leisure may be undefiled by unworthy recreation or their beauty marred by lawless pleasure. Furnish them with wings of love that they may surely and swiftly reach the heights of service, to the glory of Thy great name and the benefit of mankind; through Jesus Christ our Lord. (118)

For a Boys' School Student Body

Lord Jesus, who understandest the boy's heart, for Thou too wast once a boy, we take Thee to be our leader. Remember now Thy boyhood days and help us to master our temptations and realize our ideals. Make us lovers of our homes, loyal to our country, faithful to our God. Keep clean as a flame of fire the inner world of the heart, that our motives may be pure, our thoughts honorable, our desires manly. Encourage us to rejoice in measuring our youthful strength with hard tasks, till duty mounts into privilege and struggle into victory. Heed our aspirations; and grant that as they come from Thee as promptings, so they may return to Thee as righteous deeds, carrying on high our wills made captive to Thy service, who art the way, the truth, and the life, now and ever. (119)

For a Girls' School Student Body

O Lord, whose light doth illumine our lives as the rays of the morning sun, clothe in the radiance of purity and sincerity the youth of our land. Make the girls of this school as the polished corners of the temple. Banish aught that will tarnish the splendor or mar the beauty of their womanhood. Preserve them from the blight of worldliness, the evil of pride and vanity, the destruction of self-indulgence. Endue them with reverence, modesty, and self-control, that they may flourish like fair lilies in the courts of Thy house and shed abroad the fragrance of good works in the name and might of Jesus Christ our Savior. (120)

For a College Graduation Class

Father, we, Thy sons, gather at the beginning of our festival day to offer Thee our gratitude for having given us unremitting guidance and protection throughout the course of our college life, now at its close. Thou hast borne with our limitations, forgiven our moral lapses, and enlightened our ignorances. Be favorable to us now while we renew our pledge of loyalty to Thee and Thy teachings as we stand on the threshold of life's serious business. Enfold us with the girdle of moral purity which will tenfold increase our strength. Give us truth in the inward parts that, ridding our souls of all insincerity and deceit, we may contribute to enduring knowledge. Help us to keep inviolate our ideals that, with tireless patience and invincible courage, we may not flag in the battle of life but fight till we win. Clothe us in divinest self-forgetfulness that in our most troubled moments we may know the peace and happiness that pass all understanding. We ask Thy blessing on our Alma Mater that she may be prospered in all her undertakings and adventures for the sake of the truth that sets men free.

(121)

For a School

Spirit of Life, Counsellor of men, let Thy presence in our midst make our school a fountain of wholesome activity and true knowledge. To the Board of Governors give ripe judgment; to the masters, the gift of leadership; to the scholars, a receptive spirit, that soundness of learning, loftiness of character, and stability in vocation may be furthered to the upbuilding of Thy Kingdom, who art our God now and ever.

(122)

For Hospital Patients

Good Jesus, Physician of souls and bodies, make all sickness a healing medicine to the soul; soothe by Thy presence each ache and pain; hallow all suffering by Thine all-holy sufferings, and teach sufferers to unite their sufferings with Thine, to be hallowed by Thine. Look mercifully upon them; and, after they have suffered a little while, make them perfect: stablish, strengthen, and settle them. Hear our prayer, O Savior, who by Thy Cross and Passion hast redeemed us.

(123)

For the Grievously Afflicted

Fold in Thy compassion, loving Jesus, those who are smitten with disease. Lay a healing hand upon the wounds of their souls, that inner peace may be their portion. Revive their failing strength and let life conquer death in their suffering bodies, that rejoicing in Thy mercy they may serve Thee with grateful hearts all their days upon earth. (124)

For Physicians

O Lord, the healer of all our diseases, who knowest how the sick have need of a physician, bless all whom Thou hast called to be sharers in Thine own work of healing with health alike of body and soul, that they may learn their art in dependence upon Thee and exercise it always under Thy sanction and to Thy glory, who liveth and reigneth God forever and ever. (125)

Reverence in Dealing with Thy Handiwork

O God, of whose making and in whose keeping are the secrets of the universe, and who didst ordain man to be Lord of things created, endue such of us as tread the ways of science with reverence in dealing with Thy handiwork, and make us worthy of the great calling which bids creation yield up her treasure to our use. Unfold before our eyes the mysterious volume of Nature, that its pages may reveal Thyself in Thy works. Make known to us the processes of life wherewith we may alleviate suffering, heal the sick, and overcome the inroads of evil, that this body of our flesh may rejoice in the freedom of health as a noble vehicle of mind and a fit garment of spirit. Preside over our deliberations at this time and make us fair in argument and just in conclusions. Bend our thrones to Thy truth as Thou seest it, that we may not oppose the vagaries of self-will to the findings of true learning, but that with receptive mind, diligent hands, and trust in Thy guidance, we may play our part as fellow workers with Thee; through Jesus Christ our Lord. (126)

For Nurses

O good Jesus, who hast said, "Inasmuch as ye do it unto the least of these my brethren, ye do it unto me," look upon Thy servants who have been called by Thee to tend Thy sick and suffering children. Give them patience and tenderness, wisdom and truthfulness, and the special guidance of Thy Holy Spirit in their work, so that they may faithfully minister to those to whom Thou shalt send them, in Thee and for Thee, and may be found worthy, at the last, to receive Thine eternal reward; for Thine own merit's sake. (127)

For Dedication of a Hospital and Nurses' Home

Blessed Father, who hast promised that in every place where the remembrance of Thy name shall be put, Thou wilt come and bless us: Come now, according to Thy promise, and accept from our hands this hospital which we dedicate to Thee, beseeching Thee so to enable us to minister to the sick and suffering as to bring relief to diseased bodies and blessing and peace to distressed souls; through Him who is the great physician, Jesus Christ our Lord. The peace and blessing of God Almighty rest upon this house and upon all who shall sojourn under this roof. In the name of the Father and of the Son and of the Holy Ghost. (128)

For a Hospital Staff

O Lord, let Thy perpetual providence guide and direct the conduct of this hospital, that doctors, nurses, and pupil-nurses alike, together with the patients committed to their care, may be brought through contact with the mystery of suffering into union with Thee, where alone it is solved by the Passion, the Death, and the Resurrection of Thy Son Jesus Christ our Savior.

(129)

For Members of a Chamber of Commerce

Lord and master Workman of the universe, who hast committed to us the swift and solemn trust of life, we thank Thee for our task of weaving the threads of human affairs into the fabric of Thy purpose. Clothe us with wisdom in our stewardship as we drive the shuttle of commerce from man to man and nation to nation. May the spirit of righteousness be our guide through the entire stretch of life, in home and club, in office and factory, in work or leisure, that we may never value things above men, or surrender honor to the love of gain or the lust of power. Prosper all efforts to put an end to toil that brings no joy, and teach us how to govern the ways of industry to the hurt of none and to the benefit and prosperity of the commonwealth. (130)

For a City-wide Charity Drive

Lord of all bounty, whose tenants we are through our brief stay in the mansions of time and space, we owe it to Thee that the house of our dwelling is well-stored with good things. For the prosperity of our city we thank Thee. As stewards of Thy treasure we would ask for others the best that we ask for ourselves, and share with others the abundance with which Thou hast blessed us and our homes. We pray Thee for our fellow citizens who in the opportunities and perils of childhood, in loneliness and pain, in shame and discouragement, in age and poverty occupy our institutions or are dependent upon our care. We ask for them the sympathy and help which are richly in Thy gift. Clothe us with the spirit of generosity as we make our annual offerings to supply their need, that we may know the joy of giving, and ever maintain friendly touch with our fellows in misfortune and trial. Accept now the account of our stewardship as from those who believe in neighborliness and brotherhood, and further our charitable purpose to the advantage of this community. All of which we ask in the name of Him who taught us to pray: "Our Father. . . ." (131)

For All in High Office

Lord, be with all who are burdened with the responsibility of high office. Add the illumination of Thy counsel and wisdom to their gifts, that they may see clearly and choose the right. Deliver them from self-love, that they may be servants of all. Sustain them in the pressure of daily cares. Give them constancy and stability in the execution of their duties, that they may be true leaders of Thy people; through Jesus Christ our Lord. (132)

For the President of the United States

Almighty God, the fountain of all wisdom, guide and direct, we beseech Thee, the mind and heart of Thy servant who is called to exercise the responsibility of President of the United States. Grant that he may promote Thy will among men, the temporal and spiritual welfare of our nation, and the peace of the world. And to those who are chosen to the Cabinet give a right judgment, the spirit of courage and discretion and true godliness, to the advancement of Thy Kingdom and the benefit of our people. (133)

For the Commander in Chief, American Expeditionary Force

O God of hosts, by whose permission Thy servant John Joseph Pershing has been set over the Army of our nation, keep his heart true, his mind wise, and his hand steady. In the day of battle cover his head with Thy protection that he may lead our forces tri-

umphantly against the foe and win for the world peace
through victory, for the sake of the King of righteousness in whose name we set the battle in array. (134)

For the Induction of a Governor-General
of the Philippine Islands

O God, who supportest with Thy might these nations
of the world that look to Thee for guidance, we
rejoice in the tokens of Thy favor which have been
our portion hitherto and now since our forefathers
laid the foundation of this Republic in Thy name.
Grant that neither through the arrogance begotten of
prosperity, nor by the conceit bred of successful
achievement, may we forget our dependence upon
Thee for daily sustenance, lest we be cast from Thine
embrace into the valley of destruction. Carry us in
security to an honorable and glorious destiny. Give
to the President of the United States a prudent mind
and a strong arm, that he may be a worthy leader in
government. Cleanse the Senate and House of Repre-
sentatives from the corruption, selfishness, and injustice that desecrate our national halls, and impart to
them a heightened sense of honor to fulfil the pledges
of the nation to protect, benefit, and guide to a happy
issue the fortunes of the Filipino people. Bestow upon
Thy servant, the Governor-General of these islands,
the spirit of godliness, wisdom and might, that he
may so fulfil the high duties of office as to receive
praise of Thee. Give his fellow laborers purity of motive and unity of purpose, making them discreet in
legislation, just in administration, wise in education,

that they may be worthy instruments in carrying out Thy will. Promote among the people of the land true religion and piety, industry and prosperity, knowledge and loyalty. These and all other necessaries for them, for us, and Thy whole Church, we humbly beg in the name and mediation of Jesus Christ, our most blessed Lord and Savior. (135)

For the Archbishop of Canterbury

O God, the pastor and ruler of the people called by Thy name, look with favor on Thy servant whom Thou hast set in charge over the spiritual interests of England. Give him vision that he may inspire; wisdom that he may guide; power that he may perform. Let unity, joy, and peace evermore reign in his household until his stewardship on earth be completed to the welfare and advancement of the trust committed to his charge; through Jesus Christ our Lord. (136)

For the President of the National Organization of Churchwomen

Be Thou, O Lord, a guide and defense to Thy servant as she assumes the responsibility of high office in the Church. Give her a right judgment in all things. Inspire her with the growing consciousness of Thy benign and awful presence that with those whom she has been chosen to lead she may loyally serve the Church and reflect Thy glory among men; through Jesus Christ our Lord. (137)

For the Election of a Bishop

O God, who never failest to raise up faithful leaders
for Thy people, at this time so counsel and control the
minds of the clergy and laity of the Diocese of _____
that with clear vision they may discern the needs
of Thy Church and with unerring judgment choose
the leader Thou holdest for them in Thine eternal
counsels; through Jesus Christ our Lord. (138)

For the Church

Almighty God, without whom our labor is but lost,
prosper the work of Thy holy Church throughout the
world, O prosper Thou our handiwork. Build it upon
that foundation other than which no man can lay,
Jesus Christ. Defend it from the defilement of worldly
motives, unclean hands, and the lust of visible success, that in that day when the fire shall prove each
man's work of what sort it is, ours may abide, and we,
Thy laborers, have praise of Thee; through the same
Jesus Christ our Lord. (139)

For the General Convention of the Protestant
Episcopal Church

Be with us and in us, Holy Spirit of God, as we
gather in solemn assembly to take counsel concerning
the furtherance of Thy Kingdom that it may be on
earth even as it is in heaven. Free us from the fetters
of materialism, the blindness of prejudice, and the
disloyalty of self-seeking. Give us clearness of vision,
singleness of mind, and firmness of purpose, that,

looking not at the things which are seen but at the things which are not seen, we may courageously pursue the course of joyous obedience and loyal service. Grant this, blessed Spirit, without whom our knowledge is ignorance, our wisdom folly, and our labor lost. (140)

For a Diocese

Lord, we the clergy and people of this diocese offer Thee united praise for Thy past guidance and protection. Be with us now, as, at the dawn of a new era, we move forward to meet our new opportunities and perils. Let no problem daunt us, no failure dismay us, no success dazzle us. Build us up in Christian life and worship, that we may promote Thy Kingdom of love and righteousness; through Jesus Christ our Savior. (141)

For the Cathedral and Its Builders

O God, whose delight is among the sons of men though the heavens cannot contain Thee, establish in its strength Thy sanctuary in our midst, and make it Thy dwelling place forever. Defend under Thy wings those who labor thereon that no evil happen to them, and prosper their handiwork that a temple worthy of Thy majesty may rise to receive a people made ready for Thee; through Jesus Christ our Lord. (142)

For Missions and Missionaries

Lord Christ, to whom has been given authority over mankind and who hast made the world one neighborhood, we accept Thy sovereignty over our own lives and seek our freedom in Thy service. In a world waiting to be won for Thee, fill our souls with the joy of battle, that we may scorn fear and stand fast where need is greatest and problems thickest. Clothe us with the spirit of brotherliness, that we may share ourselves and our possessions with lavish hand among those who in far lands pace the outer wall of Thy Kingdom. Inspire us with a sense of vocation that we, looking not at things seen but at things unseen, may be builded as living stones in that eternal city of which Thou art the cornerstone, who livest and reignest with the Father and the Holy Ghost ever one God, world without end. (143)

Give of Ourselves and Our Substance

Inflame the Church of our day, O Lord, with love for Thee and obedience to Thy will, that we may freely give of ourselves and our substance to the enlightenment of the ignorant, the conversion of wrongdoers, and the building up of Thy Kingdom everywhere. Fill with love, joy, and peace our missionaries at home and abroad, that they may make fruitful barren places and the desert to blossom as a rose. Increase our laborers, multiply our givers, enlarge our gifts, that we may honor Thee and win mankind to a sincere following of Christ; through the same Jesus Christ our Lord. (144)

O God, who never failest to go with those Thou sendest, bless Thy servants whom Thou hast chosen to bear Thy name before the dwellers in the uttermost part of the earth, that they may have wisdom to know, strength to do, and patience to suffer; through Jesus Christ our Lord. (145)

For a Missionary Conference

O God, who from the beginning didst order and guide the labors of those sent forth to preach Thy Word, fail us not who aspire to evangelize the world in this generation. Grant that our deliberations may bear fruit in united effort, wise plans, and quickened love, that the knowledge of the Lord may speedily cover the earth as the waters cover the sea; for the sake of Him who is the Light of the world, Jesus Christ our Lord. (146)

For Laborers in the Harvest

O Lover of men, whose pleading voice is never silent in the souls of men, quicken the dullness of our ears to hear Thy message and obey Thy bidding. Win to Thy following the youth of our day and separate from them spiritual leaders for the work whereunto Thou hast called them. Give Thy chosen servants vivid faith wherewith to know Thee, unfeigned holiness wherewith to exemplify Thee, fiery enthusiasm wherewith to inflame their fellows, that Thy Church, being supplied with devoted priests and loyal pastors, may draw multitudes in the joy and power of Thy fellowship; through Him who is the chief Shepherd, Jesus Christ. (147)

For a National Commemoration

Almighty God and Father of all, we, Thy humble servants, implore Thy blessing upon the efforts now being made to commemorate the loving-kindness Thou hast shown Thy people in this land throughout the years that are past. Send Thy Holy Spirit upon us that all our doings may be ordered by Thy providence for the advancement of Thy Kingdom and the glory and honor of Thy holy name. Grant this, we beseech Thee, through Jesus Christ our Lord. (148)

Prayer for Sweden

O God and Father of mankind, who hast endowed nations with special gifts for the enrichment of the human race, give to the Swedish people such a sense of vocation as will enable them to develop their talents to the full. Keep aflame in them the fire of piety and devotion to Thee. Let peace reign within their borders, and righteousness and justice prevail in their institutions of government and learning. As Thou hast appointed that an assembly making for the unity of Christendom should have gathered in their capital, continue Thy favor that the reconciling influence let loose will reach the consummation in the one flock under the one Shepherd. Reward them for their hospitality and courtesy to us strangers from many lands gathered into their homes during the days of conference, and grant that they with all the nations may ever walk in the light of Thy Kingdom; through Jesus Christ our Lord. (149)

For the Unity of the Church

O God, the Father of our Lord Jesus Christ, our only Savior, the Prince of Peace; give us grace seriously to lay to heart the great dangers we are in by our unhappy divisions. Take away all hatred and prejudice, and whatsoever else may hinder us from godly union and concord: that as there is but one Body and one Spirit, and one hope of our calling, one Lord, one Faith, one Baptism, one God and Father of us all, so we may be all of one heart and of one soul, united in one holy bond of truth and peace, of faith and charity, and may with one mind and one mouth glorify Thee; through Jesus Christ our Lord. (150)

O God, who didst plan the gospel for an undivided Church, refuse not, because of the misunderstandings of its message which rend the unity of Christendom, to continue Thy saving work in the broken order of our making. Prosper the labors of all churches bearing the name of Christ and striving to further righteousness and faith in Him. Help us to place the truth above our conception of it, and joyfully to recognize the presence of Thy Holy Spirit wherever He may choose to dwell among men. Teach us wherein we are sectarian in our contentions, and give us grace humbly to confess our fault to those whom in past days our Communion has driven from its fellowship by ecclesiastical tyranny, spiritual barrenness or moral inefficiency, that we may become worthy and competent to bind up in the Church the wounds of which we are guilty, and hasten the day when there will be one fold under one Shepherd, Jesus Christ our Lord. (151)

For a Church Unity Conference

Lord Jesus, whose will it is to fold Thy flock and to make us all one in Thee, behold our earnestness to be gathered into the peace and unity of Thy appointment. Guide us who have lost our way into the path leading to Thee and to Thy purpose. Enable us, each and all, to find Thee and in Thee to find one another. Bless our efforts to follow Thy counsels and in love to reason together concerning the things that separate, to the end that, misunderstanding and self-seeking and prejudice being dispelled, we may see clearly the blessed goal and in passionate devotion pray and seek and knock until we know as we are known and love as we are loved. (152)

One Flock Under One Shepherd

Bathe with golden showers of blessing, O Lord, Thy servants whom Thy voice is calling into Thy presence to counsel with Thee concerning the peace and unity of the Church of God. Let knowledge prevail over ignorance, goodwill over prejudice, understanding over blindness, that, guided by the spirit of truth and wisdom, we may press onward with joy and confidence toward that happy day when there will be one flock under one Shepherd, Jesus Christ our Savior.
(153)

For Our Country

O Almighty and everlasting God, who, with Thy strong arm and sleepless vigilance, dost govern those nations that look to Thee for guidance, we rejoice in the tokens of Thy favor which have been our portion hitherto and now since our forefathers laid the foundations of this Republic in Thy name. Carry us, we pray Thee, in security to an honorable and glorious destiny; and grant that neither through arrogance begotten of prosperity, nor conceit bred of successful achievement, may we forget our dependence upon Thee for daily sustenance, lest we be cast from Thine embrace into the valley of destruction. To those who sit in the seats of authority impart purity of motive, right judgment in counsel, discretion in administration; to the people of the land grant loyalty, industry, and godliness, that all things may tend to the healing of division, the establishment of peace, and the promotion of Thy Kingdom among men; through Jesus Christ our Lord. (154)

For Britain and America in Wartime

O God, who didst send Thy Son into the world to share with us Thy glorious freedom, bind into a living unity the nations which claim for mankind this divine right and heritage. Give to us, the peoples of the British Empire and of the American Republic, mutual understanding and sympathy that we may press toward this common goal until victory is won, that when peace and order are restored we may together promote the coming in of Thy Kingdom among men; through Jesus Christ our Savior. (155)

For the Allied Nations During Wartime

O God, who hast promised that the kingdoms of this world shall become the Kingdom of God and of His

Christ, mightily move the Allied Nations that they may always choose Thy will as their will, Thy way as their way. So bind us together in these days of storm and battle that we may abide in perpetual fellowship through the ages to come. Let Thy strong arm help us to rise through courage to victory and win for the world that freedom which will enable the nations to bring their glory and honor into Thy Kingdom; through Jesus Christ our Lord. (156)

For Former Enemies

Lord, there is not one that doeth good, no not one. We therefore approach Thee with a sense of guilt in that however much we may think we have been wronged, we too have wronged others. However much we have to forgive, we also have much need to be forgiven. We pray Thee first to rid us of our own national arrogance, our race pride, our selfish insularity, which have made for strife and enmity in days past. Forgive our own nation, Lord, for the sins we have committed against international goodwill. Lord, we would forgive as we are forgiven. Let Thy love and compassion encompass those against whom we fought in the Great War. Heal their wounds; assuage their sufferings; right their wrongs. Unite us anew in the family of nations as companions in a common cause. For hatred give goodwill; for suspicion give trust; for aloofness give neighborliness, that we may together create that brotherhood ordained by Thee for mankind; through Him who is our great elder Brother, Jesus Christ our Lord. (157)

For Peace

Lord God of hosts, we who set the battle in array at Thy command against Thy foes and ours ascribe to Thee the victory won in Thy name and power. As Thou hast inspired us with the hope of universal peace, so guide our destiny that hope may speedily rise into fulfilment. Keep us loyal to our purpose to make the world safe for democracy and democracy safe for the world. Convert the nations that worship force and all those who exalt self above service. With the fire of divine love burn away all misunderstanding and with the bright shining of divine wisdom lighten the darkness of ignorance and error everywhere, that all nations may flow into Thy purpose as rivers flow into the sea; through Jesus Christ our Lord. (158)

O God, who hast appointed a day when the kingdoms of this world shall become the Kingdom of our Lord and of His Christ, mightily move the nations of the world that we may now and always choose Thy will as our will, Thy way as our way, Thy peace as our peace. So lock our fortunes to Thy purpose in these days of perplexity and trouble that we may reach mutual understanding and forbearance and in abiding fellowship enjoy that freedom which will enable all nations to bring their glory and honor into Thy Kingdom; through Him who came to set men free, Jesus our King. (159)

God of our forefathers, Father of the family of nations in which we claim place, as the waves of the sea unite the shores they separate, so make all the tangled web of international intercourse become the agent of goodwill and mutual understanding, to bind our strength and prosperity to the gaping wounds of the world's need. Give to our nation grace to make the high emprise of locking our fortunes to those of the family of nations bound in solemn compact to outlaw war and follow the way of order, justice, and peace, to the end that mankind may emerge from its present confusion, suspicion, and fear into the trust and gladness and power of Thy Kingdom; through Jesus Christ the Prince of Peace, our Savior. (160)

Hasten Peace

O God of Nations, who through Thy prophets of old hast foretold a day when the armaments of war shall be beaten into the implements of peace, hasten the fulfilment of this Thy most sure promise. Quell the haughty cries of the nations. Disperse the peoples that delight in war. Speedily release those who are now entangled in the net of mutual destruction, and bring us out of our present confusion into the order and righteousness of Thy Kingdom; through Jesus Christ the Prince of Peace, our Savior. (161)

For a Passion for Peace

O Lord our God, inflame our hearts with such a passion for peace which is born not of our fond desires but of Thy inflexible purpose that we may avenge the valiant dead by displacing madness by sanity, force by reason, war by law. Raise up in our midst leaders of vision and courage who, scorning peril, will guide our nation into great adventures for the well-being of mankind and the establishment of enduring peace in the whole world. Make goodwill reign in the hearts of men, and speedily bring us out of our present confusion into the order and righteousness of Thy Kingdom; through Him who is Prince of Peace and Savior, in whose name we pray, "Our Father. . . ." (162)

O Lord, give Thy tired world peace, more peace, and still more peace. (163)

For the Unity of Mankind

O Christ, who by a cross of love didst turn the counsels of sin and hate into the healing of the world, proclaim, we beseech Thee, to the peoples of the nations the things that belong to their true peace, that they may rise with a single voice to forgive past wrong, to repent present bitterness, and to remember only their unity in Thee and Thy kingdom of love, who livest with the Father and the Holy Spirit, one God, world without end. (164)

For the Conditions of Brotherhood

O Father, who art the maker and lover of the myriads of men who populate the world, arouse us to a practical belief in the full breadth of our human relationships, that we may rid ourselves of the shackles of sectionalism, national pride, and racial prejudice, and in the spirit of mutual helpfulness combine to establish those conditions of brotherhood and amity which it is our responsibility to promote. Hush the proud boastings of the nations, that they may learn to use their strength, their knowledge, their material greatness to support the weak, to enlighten the ignorant, to enrich the poor. Beat the harsh armaments of war into the kindly implements of industry and peace. Bind together the people of East and West by the ties of sympathy, respect, and service, that, in appreciation and recognition of one another's virtues and with considerate forbearance in our differences, we may be unified into one family according to Thy purpose; through Jesus Christ our Lord. (165)

3

PRAYERS FOR SPECIAL DAYS

With three counsels I would bid men to prayer:

1. Aim to see God before you address Him. In the course of time this practice will become an unbidden habit. You can see Him at least as clearly as you can the absent friend with whom you correspond, for the human lineaments are in the Divine.

2. Pray with your intelligence. Bring things to God that you have thought out and think them out again with Him. This is the secret of good judgment.

3. Repeatedly place your pet opinions and prejudices before God. He will surprise you by showing you that the best of them need refining, and some the purification of destruction.

Christmas

Father, who hast declared Thy goodwill toward us by the great gift of Thyself in the Babe of Bethlehem, grant at this Christmastide that we may receive Him with faith which adores, with love which embraces, with loyalty which follows, that, being filled with His Spirit, we may spread peace and goodwill on earth and evermore rejoice in the knowledge of Thy favor; through the same Jesus Christ our Lord. (166)

Father of mankind, who in the Babe of Bethlehem hast proclaimed to us Thy surpassing favor and goodwill, let our answering love burn with so hot a flame as to consume whatever remains within us of unworthiness of character, weakness of purpose, or unreality of motive, that, being sustained by Thy presence, we may go on our way with peace of mind and gladness of heart; through the same Jesus Christ our Savior. (167)

Good Friday

Savior, who in human flesh didst conquer tears by crying, pain by suffering, death by dying, we, Thy servants, gather before the Cross to commemorate Thy passion and to contemplate anew the wonder of Thy compassionate love. As we listen to Thy gracious words uttered with dying lips, illumine our souls that we may know the truth, melt our hearts that we may hate our sins, nerve our wills that we may do Thy bidding; to the glory of Thy name and our own eternal gain. (168)

Easter Day

O Lord Jesus Christ, Conqueror of death, Prince of life, grant that we who believe in Thy Resurrection, because we have seen Thee by faith, may so live as to witness to the power that flows from Thy presence, and by the light in our eyes and the joy in our hearts reflect faith into the souls of the doubting and the grief-stricken. (169)

Memorial Day

God of our fathers, we thank Thee for Thy providence which has guided and protected us thus far on our destiny. We acknowledge as from Thy hand the many privileges and blessings with which Thou hast showered us in bountiful abundance—the preservation of our unity, the principles of self-government, and the desire to serve the nations of the world. At this time we praise Thy holy name for all those who in sincerity and self-sacrifice have lost their lives in the service of their country. Bless and sustain their relatives. Give courage and patience to those who have been wounded and broken by war. Let ways of peace drive out ways of war. Guide and control the League of Nations in all its undertakings for peace, and bring us all at last to that happy day when war shall be no more and in mutual service the nations of the world may rise to their full stature and achieve the goal Thou hast set for mankind. (170)

Armistice Day
(now known as Veterans' Day)

We thank Thee, Lord God of hosts, as we commemorate the hour when silence fell on the battle line and the storm of warfare ceased. We acknowledge that it was Thy strong arm that enabled us to win the victory of right over wrong, and we offer Thee praise for this and all Thy benefits throughout the years of supreme world confusion, beseeching Thee speedily to establish order and goodwill among all men; through Jesus Christ our Lord. (171)

O God and Father of mankind, we gather on this sacred day to bear solemn testimony before Thee and our fellowmen to our loving gratitude for all those who, at the country's call, have met the rude shock of battle and have surrendered their lives amid the ruthless brutalities of war. We pray Thee, Lord, to grant them safe lodging in heavenly mansions and a holy rest. Forbid that their sufferings and death should be in vain; and mercifully vouchsafe that through their devotion the horrors of war may pass away from the earth and Thy Kingdom of right and honor, of peace and brotherhood, may be established among men. Comfort, O Lord, we pray Thee, all who proudly mourn the loss of those near and dear to them, especially the families of our brothers departed. Support them by Thy love. Give them faith to look beyond the troubles of this present time and to know that neither life nor death can separate us from the care of God, which is in Christ Jesus our Lord. (172)

Thanksgiving Day

O Lord of heaven and earth and sea, who givest all, with joy and gratefulness we receive from Thy bountiful hand our share in the common blessings which hourly descend upon mankind—the golden sunshine, the rain in its season, the fruit-producing soil with its flowers and trees and fields of yellow grain.

O Lord of human life, the crown and climax of things created, we acknowledge Thee as our Creator and Preserver. Our bodies came from Thy hand; and we reverence them as shrines of the mind and soul, formed for Thy use. For healthful days, for abundant joys, for our life, our gifts, our power to give, for thought and speech and motion, for the joy of worship and of service, we praise and thank Thee.

O Lord of nations, who moldest men into vast families, we own Thee as the God of our people gathered from the ends of the earth into a unity. We thank Thee for Thy benefits to us in the year past—for peace and prosperity at home, for the exaltation of righteous leaders and the confusion of evil and fraud in high places, for progress in the affairs of government, for courage in the midst of catastrophe and ruin, for guidance through the mazes of responsibility dark with perplexity.

O Lord of the Church, we thank Thee for Thine unbroken patience with the quarrels and divisions of Christendom, and for Thy continued presence in the Temple of which Jesus Christ is the Chief Cornerstone, for Thy word of truth, the sacraments of grace, the hope of glory. (173)

4

PRAYERS FROM HIS DIARY
1902-1929

God handles our affairs according to a large purpose, the whole of which, together with its beneficial and joyous issue, He sees, but only a fragmentary vision of which we can discern in the days of our mortality. Our capacity for entering into God's fuller counsels develops in proportion to our faithfulness in exercising our right of appeal. He would have us understand as far as we have wisdom to understand, and to trust where we cannot comprehend.

The first and main thing to strive for is the conviction that God's hidden activities are surer, stronger, more vitalizing than those workings of His that we succeed in deciphering; that His whole business is the management to our advantage of our concerns. Should we be inclined, under the strain of calamity in one or another of its manifold phases, to feel as though we had been neglected or our interests flouted, the history of His Son Jesus is His standing declaration that a suffering experience is the raw material out of which He can best spin the groundwork of His choicest characters. . . . Prayer is the committal of our way unto the Lord, just as a deed of trust is the committal of our possessions to those who can handle them better than we. God's response is a loyal execution of the trust by activities, hidden as well as seen. Our constant appeal to the King so works upon our personality as to make it possible for Him to control our destinies to our fullest benefit.

Prayers from His Diary

May God make me His docile, happy servant all through the unborn future. *"In la sua voluntade è nostra pace."* —1 January 1902

God be about me, before me, behind me!
—11 May 1902

May God, who puts it into my heart to be spiritual, make me strong to do as well as to desire to do.
—9 June 1902

God knows how I need transfiguring. May His mercy embrace me, His glory illumine me. —6 August 1902

O God, enable me to help some men to be what they ought to be. —20 August 1902

May God keep me loyal and empower me to do my stint of work, be the cost what it may.
—23 August 1902

May God make me a true leader of men—a leader because a true companion and servant.
—16 September 1902

Oh! I desire to do God's will: it is my purpose to do it. May He take my poor, frail will and forge it anew for the tasks undone, the battles unfought.
—19 December 1902

I long to be a braver, nobler, purer man; but I have not been ready to put my life under the discipline of the gospel. O God, turn my visions into facts, my longings into effort, my fickleness into stability.

—1 January 1903

The shattered will is powerless to respond to the calls of an awakened desire. O Lord, in Thee is my only hope. Save me from the tyranny of evil habit. Be to me a will that will shape my aspirations into a character. I crave not only pure thoughts and deeds, honesty and truthfulness in intention, but a fire of purity that burns the unclean, an honor that is instinctive, a truthfulness that is transparent. Here or there, through the disciplines of penitence and pain, by means of the purging of destruction if need be, make me clean and as Thyself. Thou art wisdom, love, and strength, and art sufficient for my ignorance, lukewarmness, and frailty.

—26 January 1903

Oh, for a higher degree of righteousness springing from the motive I preached upon—God's love, His grief when we sin, His joy when we strive. Oh, for an army of consecrated men to do the work here! Lord, enable me thus to chasten the flesh from a right motive.

—25 February 1903

O Lord, I hate sin and yet I am so miserably its unwilling victim. The things that I would not, those I do; and those that I would, I am unable to accomplish. I think I am morbidly afraid of appearing singular: O Lord, make me glad to be singular with the eccentricity of righteousness; place upon me the marks of the Lord Jesus.   —15 March 1903

O God, make me more loving, more tender, more careful of those who remain to me.—24 March 1903

O Lord, pity me and convert me by Thy Cross and Passion.   —31 March 1904

O Lord, I beseech Thee, deliver me, for I am weak. Thy hand alone can save.   —18 April 1904

May God make me patient and quiet under criticism —nay, may He enable me to profit by it.
                    —26 April 1904

Lord, deliver me from the curse of self-pity and give me courage and faith.   —28 April 1904

May God give me truth in the inward parts. May He give me courage so that I shall never play the coward and look at problems with shifting eye.—2 July 1904

May God bless these people and send laborers into this field white to the harvest.   —29 June 1905

May God help me to make the new year the best year yet.   —31 December 1905

O God, who presidest over the forces of nature, and without whose consent the earthquake and tempest cannot be loosed, manifest in the recent calamity in the homeland Thy saving love that is able to turn the shadow of death into the morning, and out of the evil work good to the lives of those who are in suffering, anxiety, or grief. Relieve the pain of the injured, turn the sorrows of those who are in suspense into joy, comfort the bereaved. Let life abound in the midst of destruction and death. Open wide the gates of Paradise to the dead and dying. To us who survive this spectacle of mortality give a sense of the impermanence of earthly things and move us to build our lives on that foundation which alone abides unmoved throughout the ages, Jesus Christ our Lord.

—April 19, 1906, *the San Francisco disaster*

O Lord Jesus Christ, I too love Thee with sincere but feeble love. Help me to deepen and strengthen my love by feeding the flock committed to my care. Grant that I may never play the part of an hireling. As a defender of the sheep I may be called to die for the sheep, which is only to play the part of a Christian. If the call comes, lead me up the slope of Calvary with strong if not joyous steps. I would follow Thee, O Lord, simply, trustfully, lovingly. My desire is to be used for eternal and undying ends. Make it my will so to be used. Lord, I embrace the cross of a swift close to life or a long waiting. Lord, into Thy hands I commend my body, soul, and spirit. Glory be to the Father, and to the Son, and to the Holy Ghost: as it was in the beginning, is now, and ever shall be, world without end.

—Lent 1908

O Jesus, who didst love Thy mother with the love of a human son, and who knowest a son's heart because Thou hast a son's heart, I thank Thee for the great mother that Thou gavest me. Her patience, her quiet courage in suffering and shame, her steadfast loyalty to her children are bright jewels that ever glisten in the setting of the past. Especially do I thank Thee for her love for me, so full of trust, so rich, so ceaseless. But, my Savior, I lament before Thee the poverty of my response to such love—my failure in tenderness, my dumbness and feebleness, the things that all unknown to her I did to shame her love. Yet I rejoice before Thee that I did not fail utterly and that my heart was loyal to her even in its worst weakness. The days are past when the arms of this flesh can enfold her. But love lives and shall live. Fill my heart with true sentiment and rich emotion for her. Let my love bear fruit in a life lived as I know she would have me live it. Let her present aspirations for me be my guide. If it is in Thy wise plan that great souls should touch us on earth from their home above, bid her lay her hand upon my head, as in the old days when I was a child, to make me a child again; and let me nestle trustfully to her bosom. Make me a child in spirit but a man in action that I may bear her a worthy record of these my latter days. And give me stalwart, homemaking love for those who are my mother's bequest to me—my dear brothers and sisters. Let any love bear fruit in high service that will not scruple to call them into the sacrifices Thou mayest beckon me to enter. And speed the day when love will divest itself of the veils of faith and hope and stand forth in its complete glory.   —Lent 1908

Lord, help me to be daring. —1 January 1909

May God make me lose self-consciousness in eager, strenuous service of the highest interests.
—11 June 1910

Lord, make me a child this year. Of such is the Kingdom of God. —1 January 1912

God does, must reign. Lord Jesus, come quickly.
—27 April 1913

May God make this new period of service more genuinely selfless and strong than any before.
—20 December 1913

O God, teach me to be increasingly stern with myself, pitiless toward my selfish desires. Make me a vigilant watchman that I may be a worthy guide.
—9 December 1914

Nearly fainted during Eucharist. Penalty of wicked worry! God forgive me. Oh, for less anxious courage!
—5 April 1914

May the kind God guide and sustain a perplexed and overborne man. —24 July 1917

May God make all my darkness as it were a candle-
stick for His light.   —14 September 1917

Lord, undertake for me. Quiet my selfish clamoring.
Be Thou my sufficiency. All things happen according
to Thy ordering. And if Thou orderest my life, there
can be no room for anything but joy when Thy de-
cree goeth forth, for Thine ordering is alone secure.
No planning or scheming of mine will mar Thy plan
for me. Nothing remains for me but to fit myself into
Thy plan. And so shall I reach my highest good and
find opportunity for my highest, fullest service. Lord,
be Thou my peace. Lay hold of my faculties and train
them to Thy use. Inspire me with undying devotion
to Thee and Thy will. I am afraid of my weakness.
Let it be a vessel to hold Thy strength. Let me not
break, O God. Fill me with divine power.
                                        —15 September 1917

Lord, I am neither brave nor good. Thou hast given
me an ideal to hold aloft and to safeguard. Grant
that my weakness may be Thy opportunity to declare
Thy power and glory. Prevent me from wavering
or falling away. If suffering be increased and failure
be my lot, yet out of my wreckage rescue the ideal
of unity and brotherhood.   —26 July 1918

God grant that we may in the end declare to all ages
the futility of force as an agent of God's Kingdom.
                                        —28 July 1918

Heavy problems and a heavy heart. Lord, help me to welcome the heavy problems in Thy name, and rid me of the heavy heart. Let me rejoice that I am still trusted with hard tasks and responsible duties. Arm me for the fight, and so relieve my conscience of the memory of past sins which weigh heavily that I may be free to give myself without distraction to my responsibilities. Make me clearheaded and stout-hearted.

—29 July 1918

O God, make me at my latter end true to the voices, voices which are the call of all the cloud of witnesses, including St. Michael and St. Katherine and St. Margaret. To be true at the end means to be true now. Often have I suppressed and disregarded the voices of God and His holy ones. Now, O God, clear the mists which obscure my soul, wrestle with and overthrow my self-will and vanity and pettiness. Give me vision and sustain me in the times when only faith is left me and I am alone yet not alone. Give to me large and enduring faith. To be without fear—this is the great thing I ask of Thee, O God.

—8 August 1918

O Lord, the heaviness of my soul crushes me. Be to me, however hidden, wisdom and strength, good Jesus. Help me to ignore all absence of happiness and peace and joy, and to do my work as though I had them. Lord, help me to rise out of the valley of self-abasement to Thy holy mount and walk with Thee. Lord, my faith turns to Thee as Savior. All

that I am, that is the vessel of the past, I commend to
Thee. Beat me into comely form upon Thy anvil.

—9 August 1918

Come what may, O God, make all and everything
the handmaid of Thy purposes and of Thy coming
Kingdom.   —11 August 1918

Lord, lift me clear of the pit of darkness by Thy love.
If I must walk in darkness, let Thy sure hand guide
me even when I think I am alone and untended. Feed
my deep inner self with Thyself and Thy life.

—26 August 1918

O God, though I am indeed unworthy to aspire so
high, I long for true service and the fulfilment of Thy
purposes.   —4 September 1918

O God, illumine with wisdom and fire and courage
my blind and fainting soul.   —28 April 1919

May God help me to be patient in suffering blame
and pain for the things known to me and unknown
which are _____'s fault. May I be like Him who
being reviled, reviled not again.   —29 April 1919

My new life, the last chapter of my life, begins now.
God make it worthy, for Jesus Christ's sake.

—16 May 1919

Lord, I would come to Thee, I, a bad child, to the perfect Child. —21 July 1919

May the good God arouse me to close-girded effort while strength remains to think and will and plan! —24 July 1919

(Nearing sunny America in a calm sea and under a cloudless sky—America with her limitless power and opportunity) —May God awaken us, her citizens, to a realization of what we may do if we will to further the commonwealth of mankind! —16 June 1923

By faith, Lord, I humbly accept Thy wonderful enrichment for which I pray. It is mine to use and to enjoy—power to love Thee with self-abandonment, to be quick to do Thy bidding, to be loyal to Thy friendship. Thy life, which is love, flows ceaselessly through me. Thou suppliest what I lack. I contemplate the actual presence within me of Thy gift. I make it my own. I go forth into the affairs of life fearlessly, for perfect love casts out all fear, victorious with the immediate victory of faith, hand in hand with Thee who walkest hand in hand with me. —3 September 1923

Lord, I receive from the fountain of Thy life, even as the babe receives milk from its mother's breast, that uprush of inner healing from the intimate withinness of Thy presence, without which I die. I ask of Thee the destruction of all barriers between my soul and

Thee, and forthwith all barriers are broken down. Thy life is mine so that I become Thine for Thy purposes. Healed at the center of my being, my infirmities and limitations become sources of power and agents of health. Lord, help me to meet the ardor of Thy giving by the ardor of my receiving, that my spiritual strength may grow with my days, to Thy honor and my salvation; through Jesus Christ our Savior.   —24 September 1923

Prayer for God's operation of love on my whole being: Lord, who is there who is not held close in Thine embrace? Those who have been most wayward and wrong are most in need of Thee. It is Thy nature to be most present where need is most. Who, Lord, more than I has need in body, mind, and spirit? Make Thy presence felt by imparting to me health and understanding and righteousness. Thou canst heal the ills of the flesh when human skill is of no avail. Lord, heal me and give me faith to accept Thy gift of health. Thou who knowest what is in man, behold my inner emptiness. Fill me with wisdom and understanding. Thou who art Spirit, breathe anew in me the breath of life, that dying I may live. Lord, hear my prayer and let my cry come unto Thee.
                              —9 September 1925

What we ask for ourselves, we pray for others as for friends and members of a common family. Awaken the great Church of Christ to new spiritual life that it may put off the tattered garments of sectarianism and clothe itself in the seamless robe of unity and fellowship. To the nations of the world give forbearance and mutual understanding that wars may cease. We pray Thee especially for our own country that we may be generous to our debtors, forgiving toward our enemies, and dauntless leaders in adventure for peace.   —1925

Last written prayer: O God, I rejoice in Thy favor. Thou hast heard my prayer and taken me unto Thy close embrace. I would set my mind on things above. Especially do I purpose to seek, in communion with Thee, new _____. I can do all things through Christ who strengtheneth me. In Thy will is my peace.
                                        —London 1929

(Bishop Brent died 27 March 1929.)

5

MY LITTLE BOOK OF PRAISE
1917-1918

The most comfortable result of a life of prayer is the security which fellowship with God imparts. His kind and cheering counsels come darting into the soul like rays of light into a dark room. Good desires increase in multitude and vigor. Unlooked-for succor rushes in to support us in moments of trial. Life expands until its branches are aflame with the sunny blossoms of hope.

Probably the greatest result of the life of prayer is an unconscious but steady growth into the knowledge of the mind of God and into conformity with His will; for after all prayer is not so much the means whereby God's will is bent to man's desires as it is that whereby man's will is bent to God's desires.

I. Thy Love

O God, I praise Thee for Thy love, that which Thou art and without which Thou couldst not be the God of man. Thy love controls and shapes Thy power so that Thy almighty hand never slips in its creative task, but makes all things well. Thy love melts Thy disciplines into the gold of spiritual treasure, and distills the soft rain of compassion from the clouds of trouble. Nothing can escape the transfiguring touch of Thy love. Under its reign the darkness becomes as the light and the unseemly face of evil flees away in shame and defeat. O God, I praise Thee for Thy love which bathes me, even me.

II. Light in Darkness

It is easy to praise Thee, O God, for the joys that flow from Thee and for Thy beauty. But in the mystery of Thy control of life there are dark places which cloud my soul. How can I make music in my heart for these? Whatever it is, it must be music of faith. The mystery is too deep for me to plumb. But Thou dost not allow evil to reign. Thine is the victory. The very wrath of man can be turned to Thy praise. Darkness and sorrow and pain may call forth a minor note, but even a sobbing song can praise Thee. Therefore, O God, I praise Thee in storm and sunshine. Praised be God.

III. Discipline

Praise God for His disciplines. It is good for me that I have been in trouble. Thy chastisement has brought me to myself, so that I can see the depth and enormity of my sin, and the height and grandeur of Thy forgiving compassion. Thy terrors have I suffered with a troubled mind, but out of the austerities of Thy love have come visions of hope and encouragement. My sin is ever before me, but of Thy mercy as forgiven sin. I praise Thee, my God, that Thou dost show me how bad I am in order that I may see how good I may be. I praise Thee that Thou dost not chastise to destroy but to build up and save to the uttermost. Behold, happy is the man whom God correcteth.

IV. The Joy of Life

All is not dark. There is always sunshine somewhere, for which I praise God—the sunshine that brightens other lives when mine is wrapped in gloom. Glory to Thee, my God, for the gladness of little children, for the joy of mothers, for the bliss of lovers. The radiance of their hearts is from Thy touch, because in the joy of Thy creation Thou rejoicest. And I praise Thee, my God, that in my unhappiest days there are breaks in the clouds through which I see the blue beyond and the glorious sun of Thy compassionate love. Even a moment of light gives me new hope and new courage to bear the stripes inflicted by my own sins. Praise the Lord.

V. The Peace of God

"O let my mouth be filled with thy praise: that I may sing of thy glory and honor all the day long." For Thy forgiveness is abundant and Thy compassion fails not. There is only one pure joy—the union of the soul with God. Praise God that He has not shut this joy from my life, but holds it out to me as a fact of the past and a promise for the future. The cloud of my sins is dispersed at the breath of His mouth and the light of His countenance. My scarlet guiltiness becomes white like the driven snow. My mouth praiseth Thee with joyful lips for the past peace, the peace of today, the coming peace that springs from sin forgiven and acceptance in the Beloved.

VI. Songs in the Night

"As for me, I will patiently abide alway: and will praise thee more and more." Even when my heart is heavy and the strings of joy will not vibrate, I can awake the music of praise with my lips. My will to praise perchance may be counted by Thee for praise when the rest of my being is dull and dim and silent. I will patiently wait for Thy reviving breath, and will praise Thee more and more with the best member that I have. Give wings to my soul, O my Praise, until it carries my whole being into the heights. My mind adds its power of thought to my will to praise and to rejoice before Thee. My emotions are silent because of my sin. I may not have the comfort of praise, but I can and will praise Thee.

119

VII. The Will

Praised be God for the power of the will. It is Thy power, and without Thee it is a menace to myself and my fellows. In its right direction is freedom. By choice we fall: by choice we rise. No choice is free unless it be guided by Thee. No choice is wise except it be inspired by Thy wisdom. I praise Thee, O God, for all the right choices I have made. I praise Thee that I can revise all the wrong choices of the past by a new and right choice. Lord, I would praise Thee by choosing right, by choosing Thee instead of me, by choosing Thy way and not mine, by choosing shame and pain if need be rather than honor and ease.

VIII. God's Long-Suffering

That God has not destroyed me in my sin is all His praise. It is of His mercy that I have not been consumed by His just anger. I merited not only His loving chastisements but the purging of destruction after the flesh. Instead of which Thou hast brought me to honor on every side. Praise God for His long-suffering. He still waits that I may praise Him by living and loving, by self-humiliation to fill the gap which He left through His forbearance. I have never waited for Thee, O God. It is Thou who art always waiting for me. Give me the grace to praise Thee with an obedient will.

IX. My Mother

Praise God for my dear and lovely mother, who bore me and bore with me and blessed me by her every thought, and for whom my own love was so flickering and unworthy. I praise Thee for showing her the fruit of her life of patient, exquisite service, and beseech Thee that I may add to lip-praise by claiming that which she coveted most for me—a meek and lowly heart and a life subordinated to Thy will. Lord, I praise Thee for sheltering her from further and perhaps deepened sorrow and suffering by taking her when and as Thou didst. I was unworthy of her; but I crave her unbroken, forgiving love.

X. My Father

Lord, I praise Thee for my gentle, kind father. He was solicitous for my welfare and loved me with tenderness. I praise Thee that no single deed of harshness or injustice mars my memory of him. Lord, fold him close to Thy mercy's breast, and give him a place near Thee that he may join in praising Thee with his redeemed life. I praise and thank Thee for the dear, earthly home in the village where I was born and bred. Recalling all its joys with gratefulness and ardent homesickness, I pray Thee to make my memory blessed to my fellow villagers.

XI. The Family in Paradise

Lord, I praise Thee for my dear brothers and sisters who live with Thee in Paradise or who still serve Thee on earth. There are the little flowers of babyhood early gathered—James, dear mother's firstborn; Herbert and sweet Ethel whose fragrance still lingers to bless my memory. Then there are my brothers for whom I might have done so much more than I did —Willoughby, the beloved physician, and Maurice, winsome boy. Eternal rest grant unto them, O Lord, and may light perpetual shine upon them. Their stains remove; their frailties do away; and fill them, O Lord, with the joy of Thy presence forevermore.

XII. My Sisters

I praise Thee, my God, for my dear sisters who are still with me in this life, and who have never given me an hour's pain, but always blessing and joy. I praise Thee for Edith, whom Thou didst lift to health from the edge of the grave and fill her with sunshine and unselfishness; for Mabel, devoted wife and mother, always loyal and true, with a Martha's hands and a Mary's soul; for Helen, with her gifts of mind and heart, a leader of others; for Evelyn, with her fragrant affection and quiet gentleness. O God, I have not deserved of Thee to be surrounded by such dear ones. But it is of Thy bounty, not my merit, that all good things have come to me.

XIII. My Fellow Workers

Lord, I praise Thee for my fellow workers, their loyalty, their affection, their trust. They have been more patient and forbearing with me than I with them. Where they have caused me anxiety and pain without my fault, I freely forgive them, and pray Thee that they may forgive me where I have in any way failed them through my ignorance, prejudice, or sinfulness. May their good works praise Thee, O Lord, and return to bless them in hours of discouragement and sadness. May their perseverance to the end crown their life of service and faith.

XIV. Opportunities

I praise Thee, my Lord God, for my opportunities of yesterday and the opportunities of today. In them I see Thee beckoning with Thy right hand and bidding me enter a door opened into heaven. Thou dost dwell in the midst of opportunity to possess it for us that we may enter in and make it our own. Yesterday I but half seized my inheritance, failing to take it by force, that Kingdom which only yields to force. Today, my God, I would praise Thee for the opportunity that gives me bruised feet and bleeding hands as I move to embrace it. Let my praise declare its measures by my fortitude and patience and loyalty even to the end. Praise the Lord.

XV. The House of My Habitation

Lord, I, a tenant at will of this Thy great universe, thank Thee, the good householder, for the place of my habitation, its beauty, its fitness, its grandeur. The land, with its fertile breast filled with rich nourishment for all creatures, praises Thee with the music and singing of myriad voices. The sea thunders forth its gladness in rolling waves. The sky with radiant face is bright with joy. Mankind adds to the chorus and thanks Thee for Thy likeness in men, for the opportunities of now and for the promise of hereafter, for the breath of life, for the light in darkness, for the conquest of death through Jesus Christ our Lord.

XVI. The Armistice

Lord, we praise Thee that Thy family, a moment since broken with hate and strife, has ceased from war. Now we wait on Thy word with sure trust that Thou wilt not leave us in disorder and confusion. Thou art forever the Creator, finding the opportunity for harmony in discord and for perfection in incompleteness. It is Thy Spirit who moves on the face of the darkness with light and wisdom in His keeping. Out of the old creation bring the new. Instill in the hearts of men a hatred of hate, and temper our justice with mercy. Thy will be done on earth as it is in heaven, for it is only in Thy will that we can inherit peace and order.

XVII. Coming Peace

The hope of perfect peace, O Prince of Peace, is most wonderful and precious. Thy peace is to be my peace.

It is a tide that is ever rising, but which can never be at the full. It wells up within and grows with our growth. The billows of a restless world swell and rage around us, but the coming peace is neither stayed nor hindered by their fury. The Kingdom within us, where Thy will reigns and which is our peace, will slowly create the Kingdom without, just as the beautiful Spirit of God breaks out in the dainty bud and the lark's glad song. Lord, I praise Thee for the peace I have and the peace I would have. Peace is not in the hushed stillness of death but in the harmony of ordered life. Lord, give Thy tired world peace, more peace, and still more peace.

XVIII. The Church

Lord, Thy bride is my mother. I praise Thee that of her is my spiritual birth. When I was a puling babe, she gathered me in her arms and presented me to Thee for safekeeping. All her precious gifts, prayer and song and sacrament, have been mine. At her bosom have I been fed with nourishment to make me strong for conflict and sure for victory. Her arms, restless with love, reach through the great world of men to gather into Thy family and hers those who are far-off and nigh. Wounded by her children, she never fails to tend and heal the wounded. Broken by angry voices within her family circle, she ever counsels peace. Shamed by rents in her beautiful seamless robe, she covers her confusion by renewed service. Lord, I praise Thee for Thy Church that is and for Thy Church that is to be.

XIX. Prayer

My Father, were it not for prayer which opens wide
the door to Thy heart, where would I be? Blessed be
Thy goodness in making it easy for Thy children to
approach Thee. Nothing human is too small for Thee
to care for. Thy understanding caress soothes every
sorrow; Thy wise counsel illumines every problem;
Thy limitless pity lightens every burden. Hence it is,
Lord, that with confidence I bring to Thee my
prattle. I ask for consolation, and Thou givest beyond
my asking; I seek for Thy wisdom, and I find Thy will
for me; I knock at the door of Thy compassion, and
Thou openest to me Thy treasure of pardon. Praise
to Thee, O God, who art ever at our call to renew
at our bidding showers of blessing.

XX. The Sacraments

The sacraments are Thyself behind a veil moving into
our lives along the path of our faith. Lord, we would
adore Thee for the stubbornness of Thy love, which
blocks every avenue of escape from Thee. Thou art
ever present, even as sunshine and air, giving us of
Thy substance without measure and without conscious intake on our part. Thou art ever coming,
ever beckoning to us to meet Thee face-to-face, ever
striving to catch our attention by inward appeal and
outward symbol. Thou art the untiring servant of the
life Thou didst create and endow with Thy likeness. Lord, I would praise Thee by more consecrated
use of the sacraments of salvation wherein Thou dost
clothe me with love.

XXI. Life in the Army

Lord, I thank Thee for my comrades in service with whom my lot has been cast in the days of war—for their brotherliness, the inspiration of their example, the splendor of their achievements. Perpetuate in peace this high privilege born of war. We bless Thee for the heroes of the wooden cross who, having made the supreme sacrifice, now reign with Thee. As they died, so let us live—to set men free. We bless and thank Thee for the uncomplaining fortitude of the maimed and wounded. Lord, be to them all that they lack. For us, who survive unharmed, provide opportunity to serve the nation with the power garnered from the red fields of battle. May our service, singleminded, stable, and fervent, be our lifelong hymn of praise for Thy preservation of us.

XXII. Hope

Now, Lord, what is my hope? Truly, my hope is even in Thee. Yea, my hope is even Thee. Thou art all promise. In the darkest night Thy star is there to cheer and guide. Hope is power to see a tomorrow containing in it more of good than the today. It is the vision of the end and some purpose of love which makes the lover and the loyal super-victors through Thee who loved us and gave Thyself for us. I thank Thee for the hope of pardon, which over and again has saved me from despair in hours of bitter self-re-proach and led me where the streams of living, cleansing water flow. I praise Thee for the hope of a better

world bound together by unity of spirit in the bond
of peace. I praise Thee for the hope that we shall
one day clearly see Thy face and share in the fullness
of Thy life.

XXIII. A Happy Day

Lord, this day has been one glad song through all
its fleeting hours. Thou hast been my near companion, pouring Thy friendship into my soul. Though
at the moment I related not always Thy gift to Thee,
now in the evening shadows in each I find Thee the
giver. Thou, the arbiter of the world which Thou
didst make, art the lover of such a least child of
Thine as I. Lord, make many the hours in which I am
conscious of Thy nearness and ministering love. Especially reveal Thyself to me in the joys and pleasures
of life that I may use them for and with Thee. Summer fades, the summer of life; and winter comes,
the winter of death. If I have learned to know Thee
in the day, I cannot fail, when night falls, to know
also that the night is Thine.

XXIV. The Chaplains' Fellowship

Thou didst found Thy Church, O God, on the foundation of fellowship—the glorious company of the
Apostles, the goodly fellowship of the Prophets, the
noble army of Martyrs. And always Thou Thyself hast
been the foremost companion and friend. For this
towering boon in a world of benefits I praise Thee,
who hast called me to share in the fellowship we

build, our Chaplains' Fellowship. Lord, we thank
Thee for the unity of understanding and service in
our life as chaplains. As Thou hast brought us to
know one another during the strain and horror of
war, so hold us in the calm and happy activities of
peace, that we may bring order and new power into
Thy holy Church throughout all the world. We
praise Thee, O social, friendly Lord.

XXV. Deserved Suffering

"What glory is it, if, when ye sin, and are buffeted
for it, ye shall take it patiently?" It is of Thy mercy,
my righteous and loving judge, that Thou dost not
abate Thy chastisement for my sins. Thy lash is the
lash of love; therefore, it is my simple duty to praise
Thee even when the pain of punishment is sore. Sin
is disease: punishment is remedy. I praise Thee for
the fitness of all the disciplines which have followed
on my trespasses. Lord, help me not to fear them but
to embrace them and to kiss the cross of Thy loving
justice. I would pray Thee for one favor—that the
penalties that are wholly mine should not be visited
on others to their hurt. If they, too, must share inno-
cently what I bear justly, let mystic power transfigure
their pain until there comes to them clear shining
after rain.

XXVI. Undeserved Suffering

"This is thankworthy, if a man for conscience toward
God endure grief, suffering wrongfully . . . if, when
ye do well, and suffer for it, ye take it patiently, this

129

is acceptable with God." I do thank Thee, my God, for opportunity to bear pain for others. Father, forgive them: they know not what they do. I praise Thee for giving me this opening to exercise forgiving love. Grant that I may shield those who have been unfair to me and to take with quiet thankfulness and open arms the humiliation that may come for the sake of Him who His own Self bare our sins in His body upon the tree. That suffering, O Christ of the Agony, is in itself conquest and victory. Whatever place in my life it may have, I rejoice for it and praise Thee for it. Keep me steadfast that I may not fall into the trap of self-justification.

EDITOR'S NOTES

1. PRAYERS FOR PERSONAL NEEDS

1   *1905 Notebook.* This prayer was printed by S. S. Drury in *Adventures in Prayer* (1932), p. 5, in the following version: "O God, who wakenest sleeping night with the magic touch of dawn, lay Thy morning hand on all my faculties which sleep and fill them with the light of Thy life; through Jesus Christ our Lord."

35   24 May 1922
36   1907
37   1908
38   1916
39   16 June 1923
40   22 February 1925
41   *1926 Notebook*
42–43   Lent 1908
44   Undated
45–46   21 May 1922
47   February 1926
48   16 November 1924
49   *1905 Notebook*
50–51   Philippines
52–54   Lent 1908
55   Philippines
56   February 1926
57   Before 1916
58   Philippines
59   *1905 Notebook*
60   26 May 1922
61   Ascension Day 1922
62   *1905 Notebook*
63–64   Undated
65   20 May 1922
66   11 August 1924
67   *1905 Notebook*
68   Lent 1908
69   Undated
70   *1905 Notebook*
71   3 January 1922
72   20 May 1922
73   28 February 1925. Adapted from Bishop
          Hacket, seventh century
74   19 November 1922
75–77   1908

78–82   Undated
83   This prayer is an illustration of the way in which Bishop Brent combined parts of old prayers for special occasions. Here he fuses elements of St. Francis' *Canticle*, his own evening prayer, and a prayer book collect. This prayer was used at an evening service aboard the *S. S. Leviathan* on 20 February 1919.
84   Undated
85   Philippines
86   1906
87   Undated
88–89   *1905 Notebook*
90   Epiphany 1925
91   Undated
92   Final version of prayer composed in the Philippines found on p. 83 of Drury, *op. cit.*
93   Undated

2. Prayers for Persons, Occasions, and Causes

94   31 January 1929
95   Philippines
96   24 May 1922
97   Philippines
98   *1905 Notebook*
99–100   Undated
101   *1905 Notebook*
102–105   Philippines
106   J. P. Morgan was the specific steward of wealth named in the original prayer.
107–109   Philippines
110–111   Undated
112–114   1910
115–116   Undated

117	Written for dedication of Children's Corner in Church of the Epiphany, Rochester, N. Y., on Quinquagesima, 27 March 1927
118	2 September 1922
119	Philippines
120	18 November 1904
121	21 June 1927, Harvard University
122–125	Undated
126	20 February 1926
127–129	The University Hospital and Nurses' House, All Saints' Day 1909
130	1925
131	Undated
132	*1918 Notebook*
133	For Herbert Clark Hoover
134	*1918 Notebook.* Bishop Brent confirmed General Pershing in Manila on 23 January 1910.
135	Philippines
136	On occasion of enthronement of the Most Rev. and Rt. Hon. Randall Davidson as 96th Archbishop of Canterbury, 1903
137–138	Undated
139	Undated final version of prayer originally composed in Philippines, early draft of which appears in Drury, *op. cit.,* p. 52
140	Written aboard *S. S. Drottningholm* on 11 September 1925
141	1919
142	Philippines
143	1925
144	Centenary of the Domestic and Foreign Missionary Society
145	*1905 Notebook*
146	1910. The following is another version (undated) of this prayer: "O Spirit of God, who from the beginning didst order and guide the

labors of those sent forth to preach Thy Word, fail us not who aspire to pray as our Savior prayed that we may all be one. Evangelize the world before the night falls in which no man can work. Fill us with that vivid expectancy which moved the waiting disciples in the infant church till Pentecost was fully come. Grant that our deliberation may bear fruit in united effort, wise plans, and quickened love, that the knowledge of the Lord may speedily cover the earth as the waters cover the sea; for the sake of Him who is the Light of the world, Jesus Christ our Savior."

147   Autumn 1918

148   Canadian Bi-Centenary, 1910

149   7 September, aboard *S. S. Drottningholm* en route Universal Conference on Life and Work, Stockholm, 1925

150   Undated

151   Drury, *op. cit.*, p. 53. The following is an early version of this prayer: "O God, who madest the gospel for a united Church, refuse not, because of our misunderstandings of its message and the dissensions that rend the oneness of Christendom, to continue Thy saving work in the broken order of our making. Bless the labors of all churches bearing the name of Christ and striving to further righteousness and faith in Him. Show us wherein we are sectarian in our contentions, and give us grace humbly to confess our fault to those whom in past years our Communion has driven from its fellowship by ecclesiastical tyranny, spiritual barrenness, or moral inefficiency, that we may become worthy and competent to bind up in the Church the wounds of which we

135

are guilty. Help us to place the truth above
our conception of it, joyfully to recognize
the presence of Thy Holy Spirit wherever He
may choose to dwell among men. Endue us
with the mind of Christ, that we may all become one in Him."

3. PRAYERS FOR SPECIAL DAYS

4. PRAYERS FROM HIS DIARY

These prayers were all extracted from Bishop Brent's
diaries for the years 1902–1929.

5. MY LITTLE BOOK OF PRAISE
1917–1918

Among the literary remains of Bishop Brent was found
a pocket-size notebook, bound in black leather, of the

type readily obtainable in any stationery store, on the flyleaf of which Bishop Brent had written:

1917–1918

MY LITTLE BOOK OF PRAISE

C. H. Brent

The notebook contained twenty-six meditations, each titled and each an exact page in length, in the Bishop's handwriting. That he planned for forty-four meditations is indicated by the Roman numerals placed in advance at the head of unfilled pages. So far as can be ascertained, these meditations were written while Bishop Brent was on duty on the Western Front as Senior Headquarters Chaplain, that is, Chief of Chaplains, American Expeditionary Force, 1917–1919.

1862	Born April 9 in Newcastle, Ontario, Canada, son of the Reverend Canon Henry Brent and Sophia Frances (Cummings) Brent.
1880–1882	Student, Trinity College School, Port Hope, Ontario.
1884	Bachelor of Arts with honors in classics, Trinity College, University of Toronto.
1884–1886	Member of faculty, Trinity College School.
1886	Ordained Deacon March 21 by Bishop Sweatman of Toronto.
1886–1887	Curate and organist, St. John's Church, Buffalo, N. Y.
1887	Elevated to Priesthood by Bishop Sweatman in Toronto.
1887–1888	On staff of St. Paul's Church (now Cathedral), Buffalo, N. Y., in charge of St. Andrew's Mission.
1888–1891	With Cowley Fathers (Society of St. John the Evangelist) in Boston, Massachusetts, and priest-in-charge, St. Augustine's Mission for Negroes.
1889	Master of Arts, Trinity College, University of Toronto.
1891	Became United States citizen; in November made first ocean voyage to England.
1891–1901	Associate Rector (Rector, last two months) of St. Stephen's Church, Boston, Massachusetts.
1899	First book published—*With God in the World*.
1901	Elected first Missionary Bishop of the Philippines October 11; accepted election November 15; consecrated December 19.
1901–1918	Philippine Episcopate.
1902	Sailed for Philippines in May via Rome and Suez.

1903–1904	Member of committee appointed by Philippine Government for investigation of opium problem in the Orient.
1904	Paddock Lecturer, General Theological Seminary, New York City.
1907	William Belden Noble Lecturer, Harvard University.
1909	Chief Commissioner for United States and President of First International Opium Conference at Shanghai.
1910	Attended Edinburgh, Scotland, International Missionary Conference, where he conceived idea of a World Conference on Faith and Order.
1911	President, Second International Opium Conference, The Hague.
1917–1919	Senior Headquarters Chaplain, American Expeditionary Force.
1917	Elected fourth Bishop of Western New York —October 2.
1918	Became Diocesan January 19.
1919	On February 6 began diocesan duties.
1920	Chairman of meeting at Geneva, Switzerland, to plan World Conference on Faith and Order.
1921	Delivered Duff Lectures at Edinburgh, Glasgow, and Aberdeen Universities.
1923	U.S.A. Representative on Advisory Committee on Narcotics of the League of Nations.
1924	U.S.A. Representative at International Opium Conference, Geneva, Switzerland.
1925	Delegate to Universal Christian Conference on Life and Work, Stockholm, Sweden.
1926–1928	Bishop in charge of the American Episcopal Churches in Europe.

1927 President, First World Conference on Faith and Order, Lausanne, Switzerland, August 3-21.

1928 To London November 3 for Canterbury functions attendant upon retirement of Archbishop Davidson and enthronement of Cosmo Gordon Lang as Archbishop of Canterbury.

1929 Died, March 27, in Lausanne, Switzerland where buried in Bois de Vaux Cemetery.

HONORARY DEGREES AND DECORATIONS

Doctor of Divinity: University of Toronto, 1901; University of King's College, Halifax, Nova Scotia, 1911; Yale University, 1919; University of Glasgow, 1920; Trinity College, Hartford, Connecticut, 1920.

Doctor of Sacred Theology: Harvard University, 1913; Columbia University, 1917.

Doctor of Laws: Columbia University, 1920; University of Rochester, 1922; Union College, 1924; University of Toronto, 1924; New York University, 1925.

Commander of the Order of Leopold (Belgium).

Officer of the Legion of Honor (France).

Companion of the Order of the Bath (Great Britain).

Distinguished Service Medal (United States of America).